ESCAPE TO
HOLLYWOOD

LIDIA LUKES-HITCHCOCK

WRITTEN WITH **GARETH OWEN**

Escape to Hollywood
Published in 2025 by
Oak Tree Books
West Wing Studios
Unit 166, The Mall
Luton, LU1 2TL
oaktreebooks.uk

Copyright © 2025 Lidia Lukes-Hitchcock

The right of Lidia Lukes-Hitchcock to be identified as author of this work has been asserted in accordance with the Copyright, Designs and Patents Act 1988.

All rights reserved. No reproduction, copy or transmission of this publication may be made without express prior written permission. No paragraph of this publication may be reproduced, copied or transmitted except with express prior written permission or in accordance with the provisions of the Copyright Act 1956 (as amended). Any person who commits any unauthorised act in relation to this publication may be liable to criminal prosecution and civil claims for damage.

The views and opinions expressed herein belong to the author and do not necessarily reflect those of Oak Tree Books or Andrews UK Limited.

For Paul

Following the coup d'état of February 1948, the Communist Party of Czechoslovakia seized power in the country with the support of the Soviet Union and declared it a socialist republic.

The country effectively became a communist satellite state under Soviet rule.

For five decades, widespread nationalisation, repression of dissidents and show trials ensued.

With the fall of the Berlin Wall in 1989, things began to change, but up until then it had been a feared and strictly controlled regime which many ordinary people hoped to escape.

This is the story of one woman who did escape to build a new life and career in London. Her daring journey to the West was all sparked by Hollywood legend Barbra Streisand!

CONTENTS

FOREWORD   1

CHAPTER 1
Barbra   4

CHAPTER 2
Growing Up   8

CHAPTER 3
Escape – Part One   24

CHAPTER 4
Escape – Part Two   32

CHAPTER 5
Reunited   47

CHAPTER 6
The Typist   58

CHAPTER 7
Warner Bros.   64

CHAPTER 8
Stanley Kubrick   72

CHAPTER 9
First Knight   82

CHAPTER 10
Terminal Velocity   119

CHAPTER 11
Mission: Impossible   123

CHAPTER 12
The Saint   135

CHAPTER 13
The Man In The Iron Mask 148

CHAPTER 14
Castaway & Vertical Limit 155

CHAPTER 15
Mission Impossible II 160

CHAPTER 16
Providing Product Placement 176

CHAPTER 17
Fred Claus 182

CHAPTER 18
Paul 189

CHAPTER 19
It's A Wrap! 200

FILMOGRAPHY 203
ACKNOWLEDGEMENTS 205

FOREWORD

You think you know someone until you read their candid, and in this case, delightful memoir.

Lidia and I became acquainted in 1995 as we were both hired by Paramount Pictures to work on the very first of the Tom Cruise MISSION: IMPOSSIBLE movies. It was the first big-budget international production to attempt to film in Prague in the recently created Czech Republic. Democracy was relatively new and the country had no bureaucratic template to handle the fast-paced demands of a production of this scale. Lidia, Czechoslovakian by birth but living in London, was just the person to return to her home country to help facilitate the many negotiations and soothe sceptical nerves. Smart, industrious, and opinionated, she proved to be the consummate problem-solver.

As sometimes happens on film shoots, a friendship began which has lasted now 30 years. That friendship has revealed other qualities that have transcended the professional experience – generosity, sensitivity, and a sense of humour that sometimes I think she is unaware of!!

To be with Lidia is to laugh. Ours was not the most important friendship that blossomed for Lidia during the filming, but no spoilers will be revealed here.

ESCAPE TO HOLLYWOOD is a story of determination and luck, of escape and reinvention, of a journey quite impossible. One does not have to have met Lidia personally to be inspired by the life events revealed.

Most of all it is a love story.

Consider this an introduction, both literally and figuratively. Get to know Lidia and let her well-told tale envelop you. As it did me.

Chris Soldo
Producer / Director/ First Assistant Director
LA, June 2025

PART ONE
THE EAST

CHAPTER 1

Barbra

In early 1980s Czechoslovakia we were at the peak of communism, and I hated it – I hated what the country had become, I hated the restrictions imposed upon us, and I hated Soviet economic and political ideology. Yet perversely, it was the only life I had ever known, having been born in 1947 just after the end of World War II. Though my parents used to tell me of their earlier lives, which seemed so full of opportunity and optimism before the war, I wondered if I might ever experience even a hint of that fairytale-like existence.

It wasn't that we were a poor family living in the drab, grey conditions that you often saw in Western-made Soviet-era dramas and movies; no, we lived quite comfortably, and from 1976 I had been employed at Barrandov Studios working on many Czech and Russian films, first as an assistant, then coordinator and finally as production manager. Yes, it's true shops did not have a wide array of food and comestibles, but we wanted for little. I also undertook occasional work on German, Austrian and French international productions, which proved an exciting and enjoyable diversion, and which allowed me to gain experience of international movies which so often visited for location work, utilising our wonderful castles, ancient streets and unique landscapes. By far the most important of these visiting productions, to me at least, was an American film called *Yentl* (1983). That one film not only became the turning point in my career, but the catalyst for what was to follow – my daring escape to the West.

In 1968, Barbra Streisand had enjoyed great success when the movie *Funny Girl* won her an Oscar and the world was, figuratively, at her feet. After reading Isaac Bashevis Singer's book 'Yentl: The Yeshiva Boy', she decided it would be her next project.

The story was set in 1904 and centred on a 16-year-old Ashkenazi Jewish woman in Poland who decided to disguise herself as a man so she could receive an education in Talmudic law. Study of the Babylonian Talmud – which underpinned Jewish life, law and scholarship for centuries – was almost exclusively studied by men, and the idea that women might study it was frowned upon and still is in some areas even today.

It took years for Barbra to get the film off the ground, which I'll come to later, but in 1982 she arrived in Prague to start planning its production, after several earlier trips to recce possible locations. I didn't really speak much English, so we had interpreters assigned to work between us ('us' being the Czech production partner) and the American delegation. Of course, the interpreters were all working for ŠtB, the Secret Police, so we had to be guarded in what we said and discussed. One of them, who was assigned to Barbra Streisand personally, was quite a nice lady – relative to the others – and I befriended her a little.

There was then only one decent hotel in Prague, the Intercontinental; the others were all communist constructed blocks that were pretty horrid, brutalist-looking places usually favoured by Russian diplomats. There were not that many Western tourists in Prague during the communist era, yet almost all the hotels, which were operated by a state-controlled chain, had tourist-friendly names. Behind the façades, however, lay cheerless, cold and stark Interior Ministry accommodation.

Barbra requested the presidential suite at the Intercontinental for her two-week stay, as it was befitting her status, though on her arrival she was suddenly informed that the suite was no longer available and she had instead been allocated the floor below, with several connecting rooms.

Barbra was clearly not happy, and whilst she didn't quite throw a tantrum, her expression said it all. I quickly stepped in and asked the 'friendly' interpreter what had happened, as I understood it had all been agreed, and of course, Barbra was paying top dollar too. I laid it on pretty thick, saying we must realise that Barbra Streisand was a big Hollywood star, with an important movie, and was bringing a big American spend into the country... and so on.

The interpreter, realising that I was getting perhaps a little too animated on Barbra's behalf, took me to one side and said quietly, 'It is because the bugs in the Presidential Suite are not working.'

I don't suppose I was surprised, but I knew I had to warn Barbra. I couldn't be seen to say anything against the state, of course, as it would place me in great personal danger, but with my very basic English, I was able to alert Barbra when no one was looking, 'Do not say anything in those rooms. They will be listening.'

Barbra realised she had an ally in me, and we got on very well from that moment, despite the language barriers. In fact, a few days into her stay, she called me very early one morning at home, around 5.30am. She was quite pedantic in that when she visited certain locations, she always wanted to wear the costume associated with the scenes in the script and have the music playing from a tape machine. On this particular morning, we were scheduled to visit a synagogue at 7.30am and Barbra needed to clip back her hair for the character's wig to be fitted, but she panicked when she realised she didn't have any hairpins. They didn't have any at the hotel, and with dawn hardly broken, there was nowhere else for her to get any.

I instinctively said, 'Don't worry! I will be there in 30 minutes,' not really knowing what I was going to do, but in the film business I had learned never to say no to anything – there was always a solution, even if you didn't know what it might be.

I phoned and woke up my hairdresser. 'Romanka, I need you to go to your salon now, and I need a handful of hairpins. It's very important.'

Fifteen minutes later, I was there, picked up the clips, jumped onto the tram and arrived at the Intercontinental by 6am to meet the eternally grateful star. From that point, whatever Barbra needed or asked for, I got it, and you must remember it wasn't always easy to get hold of things in communist Prague. Barbra was always grateful and, in fact, said, 'Lidia, after we have made this film, you will come back to Hollywood and work for me.'

I was genuinely taken aback. Rarely did any producers ever thank you, let alone make you an offer like that!

At the end of her stay, Barbra felt Prague was ideal, 'The locations are perfect, and I love it here, but when I come back, I would like you to have learnt better English so that we can talk about everything without the need of a translator.'

I immediately enrolled in classes and learned better English – I'm still learning to this day, in fact!

I knew if my career was to progress, then I needed to leave Czechoslovakia and learning English would, of course, be to my advantage – and with the instruction coming from Barbra to take lessons, it seemed the perfect excuse and wouldn't arouse any undue suspicion.

But getting out of the country was far from straightforward, with ŠtB/Secret Police spies everywhere and strict travel restrictions imposed, meaning only one family member could travel at a time, and never, ever could family members travel together outside the country to the West. Any flaunting of the rules was met with imprisonment, if not worse, and as I had a teenage son, I knew escape without him didn't bear thinking about, but escaping with him was impossible. Or was it? I had learned never to say no to anything, remember… and so began a plan, which took three years to painstakingly put together, and which transported me to the UK, Hollywood and beyond, working with such stars as Tom Cruise, Sean Connery, Richard Gere, Cindy Crawford, Jon Voight, Tom Hanks, Anthony Hopkins, Leonardo DiCaprio, Val Kilmer, and directors like Stanley Kubrick, Christopher Nolan, Robert Zemeckis, John Woo and many others.

I could never have dreamed of such a wonderful life and career; however, my journey proved dangerous, risky and was pitted against all the odds.

CHAPTER 2

Growing Up

As mentioned, I arrived in 1947 – exactly a year after my parents married.

My father, Jaroslav, was born in Czechoslovakia in 1913 and after leaving school in 1929 he travelled to Switzerland to study hospitality– to this day the country still boasts the very best training colleges in the business – and in 1932 aged 19, he found himself working in Berlin in the fashionable district of Unter Den Linden, just as Nazism began sweeping across the country. A few months later, Adolph Hitler came to power, and although my father wasn't in any immediate danger, he was 'involuntarily kept' in Germany with his passport confiscated. He remained and worked there until the end of World War Two. When what was left of the German Army surrendered, and the final German resistance had been worn down, my father discovered his was the only building standing on that side of the street – the Allies had flattened a lot of Berlin by aerial bombardment and had he been in a building opposite, I wouldn't be here today.

Dad packed up his meagre belongings and stuffed all the money he'd saved up into a shoe box before setting off on his long journey home to Prague.

It took him two months in all: walking, hitchhiking and by whatever other mode of transport he could blag his way on, until he arrived at my grandparents' house and collapsed into their arms, utterly exhausted. They were so overwhelmed at seeing their son after so many years of not hearing from him or even knowing if he was alive or not, that they just burst into tears.

I wish I had known more about my father's younger days, his time in Germany and his eventful journey home, but aside from a few brief mentions here and there he completely refused to talk about it; I can only imagine he was so traumatised and mentally scarred by all he witnessed and his virtual imprisonment that it would have been so very painful for him to recall. Though he did keep the shoe box full of Deutschmarks (or rather Reichsmarks) he'd carried with him, and I often took it out of the wardrobe as a young child to marvel at the one-hundred thousand and one million bank notes, thinking we were millionaires – the currency had become so inflated that cigarettes were more valuable, and by 1948 the Reichsmark was considered totally worthless.

My mum, Jolana, meanwhile, was born in Hungary in a town just on the border with Slovakia. After the war, my mother was given the opportunity to move to the Sudetenland, a province in northern Czechoslovakia, bordering Germany, which the Nazis had seized. The area had long been desired by the Third Reich not only for its land mass but also because a majority of its inhabitants were considered 'ethnically' German, and in the summer of 1938, Hitler had demanded its annexation, aware that the Allies were so desperate to avoid war that they'd likely appease his demands. When British, Italian, French and German leaders met in Munich, the Allies unanimously agreed to concede the territory in exchange for a pledge of peace, known as the Munich Pact. But neither the Czech government nor its people were consulted or invited to the discussions, and in response, the democratic government of my country resigned.

Less than six months later, Hitler broke the Munich Pact and invaded the Czech provinces of Bohemia and Moravia, which were immediately placed under Nazi rule. Following that move, Hungary made territorial claims on the south of what was formerly Czechoslovakia, resulting in the country (as people had known it) all but disappearing from the map.

At the end of the war, when Czechoslovakia was reconstituted, the Sudeten Germans were expelled and the Czechs were not keen on returning to the then desolate area, but my mother saw it as an opportunity and a stepping stone. She settled there for around three months before, in the autumn of 1945, moving to Prague and gaining work at a factory there. She met my father soon after, at a Sunday afternoon dance.

In January 1946, they were married!

Sadly, my father suffered heart problems and in 1965, aged just fifty-one, he succumbed to a huge heart attack. His untimely passing left a huge hole in our lives, and I can't help but feel that the time he was forced to stay and work in Germany had a hugely detrimental effect on his health. It had also instilled in him a deep-rooted hatred of dictatorship – and in our case, that meant communism.

***

Later that year, I graduated from high school and had ambitions to go on to university, but my mother reluctantly said she couldn't afford to support me through three more years of education, and in fact really needed me to bring in a salary to the house if we were going to be able to make ends meet.

I had no idea what I wanted to do in life, let alone as a career, but Mum – being as practical and industrious as always – said, 'OK, I will find you a job.' I think that was a Thursday, and she returned home a couple of hours later, telling me I was set to start work the following Monday. I sort of panicked, thinking I had only a few days of freedom left – it seemed like a pending sentence rather than a new chapter of my life.

If there was one subject I hated, and was useless at, it was mathematics. You might therefore find it somewhat surprising to learn that on the following fateful Monday, I reported for duty in a bank – how they even considered me, let alone accepted me, was surely a testament to my mother's persuasive skills!

My duties were mainly in administration, such as checking statements and the like 'behind the scenes'. I suppose they at least had the good sense not to put me in a customer-facing role, as my total disinterest wouldn't have reflected well on, or instilled any confidence in, my employers.

I remained quite pragmatic in that, although I hated the job, I looked upon it as being a way of buying me some time to really figure out what I wanted to do with my life, whilst bringing in some money to help my mother.

Along the way, I met a young man named Oli who became my first boyfriend.

***

For a few fleeting months in 1968, Czechs living under Communism got to enjoy newfound freedoms and reforms in a period known as the 'Prague Spring' thanks to Alexander Dubček, the First Secretary of the Presidium of the Central Committee of the Communist Party of Czechoslovakia.

That was until August 21st, 1968, when Dubček's proposed democratic reforms had alarmed the Kremlin and resulted in the overnight invasion of the country, with tanks from the Soviet Union moving in. All of the important government buildings, airports, railway stations, along with newspapers, radio and TV broadcasters were immediately seized and taken over. My mother woke me up at 5am with tears in her eyes – this was the first time I had ever seen her cry, so I immediately leapt out of bed.

'What happened? Mum, what is wrong?' I cried out.

She led me to the window, pulled back the curtains and pointed ... 'We've been invaded,' she said.

'Invaded? What do you mean?'

I looked at the river embankment opposite and saw rows and rows of tanks and military vehicles lined up, with their guns pointing inwards at Prague.

Overnight, Czechoslovakia had moved very firmly back under total Soviet control and despite us switching on the radio for news, it all seemed chaotic and confused – no one really knew what was happening to be honest; on one frequency the state broadcaster was calmly reporting that we had been 'liberated', but in retuning, my mother happened upon other voices, desperately reporting that this was an out-and-out invasion and all our liberties were being removed, and that we should stay indoors. It was totally terrifying.

I didn't dare to go out that day but did watch the many soldiers and artillery moving into Prague from every direction, wondering what might become of us.

By the next day, we were actually encouraged to go back to work and to follow our normal routine, but how could anything be normal when you had to walk past armed soldiers on every street corner and when main roads had cordons across them?

My boyfriend Oli came to our apartment with the news that borders were going to open for one week, and one week only, for anyone who wanted to leave. He said he was going to Austria and wanted me to go with him. I suddenly felt very torn; yes, I wanted to be with Oli, but how could I possibly leave my mother at that time of great uncertainty, especially as she was now a widow with no other family. It was just impossible, but I understood this was perhaps the only chance Oli would have to escape what was sure to be dreadfully repressive years ahead.

When the day came, we said our goodbyes, though Oli remained ever-hopeful I might change my mind at the last minute. Whilst there was no way I could, I do believe it sowed the seed of needing to get out of the country.

Life became more suppressed, with shops increasingly devoid of food and other goods, whilst the visibility of Russian soldiers and their families increased, which also contributed to the growing shortages. It was a situation we did not take easily to, but there was no way to protest because anyone who did ended up in prison.

On the rebound from Oli, I met a man named Tony. We fell in love and married. You can guess it wasn't a basis for a long and strong marriage.

***

On March 28, 1969, in a rare display of nationalistic and anti-Soviet feeling, the Czechoslovak national ice hockey team defeated the Soviets at the world championships in Stockholm (where they had been moved from Prague). Czech people watched it eagerly on TV and throughout the country took to the streets celebrating the victory, often taunting the Soviet occupiers and venting resentment in a massive, nationwide celebration. At last, the worm had turned.

Tony and I joined the crowds on Wenceslas Square in the centre of Prague who were protesting against the Soviet military.

I did not know why we were there if I'm honest, but it was a sudden urge en masse to participate in a demonstration of our true feelings – at long last. What was I thinking of? What was I doing? I was 4 months pregnant! Though it did not show much, and thinking back now, if I had any sense, I should have been sitting at home with my feet up.

It all started very innocently, with like-minded people coming to the square in the belief our voices would be heard and hoping the size of the crowds would be enough to bring about a peaceful change. Then, suddenly, somebody threw bricks into the office of Aeroflot (the Soviet national airline) and others ran in to ransack it. At that moment, the military and police, who were obviously prepared and waiting, cordoned off the whole square – there was no visible escape. Tony and I grabbed each other, scared at what was happening around us, when suddenly a guy and his girlfriend nearby gestured to us.

'Quick, I know a passageway which might not be blocked,' he said, and we followed. True, we did make a lucky escape, but when I arrived home later, I was shaking and started to cry uncontrollably. It dawned on me how reckless we had been, but then again, I felt we were actually part of something important that was brewing.

I heard the following day on the radio that many people from the protest were taken to prison. Of course, that news was used as a pretext to oust the remaining leaders of Prague Spring – among them, Alexander Dubček. He was sidelined and his reforms were all reversed – mainly by those inside the party who benefited most from the Stalinist economy and institutional power.

During the later Velvet Revolution of 1989, Dubček served as the Chairman of the federal Czechoslovak parliament and contended for the presidency alongside Václav Havel.

But it was not to be.

Dubček died in a car crash in 1992, when he was the odds-on favourite to become the President of the newly independent Slovak Republic. The crash was treated as suspicious, but nothing was ever proved, with the investigation concluding that the high speed of the driver in heavy rain was to blame. Dubček's car was destroyed shortly after the crash, and it later emerged that the driver was part of the ŠtB.

Happily, our son, Martin, was born in August 1969, and from the June prior, I was able to take maternity leave from my job – at last I was free of the damn bank, I thought. Well, for six months at least.

We soon realised little Martin had severe eczema, and it really plagued his early life with visits to many doctors, several hospitals and trials of various creams, lotions and other medication, throughout which he suffered great discomfort and pain. I knew that I needed to be a 'stay at home' mum to be able to look after Martin, taking him to his many appointments, and it would have proven impossible for him to be left at a creche, knowing about the one-on-one care he often required.

Unusually for the communist state, whose mantra was that everyone should work regardless of any disability or problem, they took a very lenient view of us. It wasn't easy, particularly financially, but when we eventually found a treatment that worked for Martin, he was around three years old and was finally able to join a nursery and begin living a more normal life with his peers.

Martin's improved health meant I also needed to return to work, and in 1973, I answered an advert to join a cosmetic company called Dermacol, which was linked with Max Factor and had offices at Barrandov Studios. In fact, they had a whole building there, which suited me as my husband Tony worked in the sound department. Dermacol, incidentally, was (and still is) the leading Czech manufacturer and seller of make-up and decorative and skin cosmetics, which was founded in Prague in 1966. Three years later, film studios in Hollywood bought a license to produce high cover makeup from the company, which they found perfect in covering any blemishes or imperfections in their stars' skin tones.

I applied and was invited for an interview. The boss was a Mr Ing Boublik, a very charming, entrepreneurial gentleman who told me he was really looking for an all-round secretary.

'Can you type?' he asked.

I paused for a second before confirming, 'Yes, I can.'

Actually, I had never used a typewriter in my life.

'Okay, I'll dictate something, and you type it up …'

This very same thing happened at a later job interview in London and then, just as here, I knew I'd barely be able to type a line let alone a whole letter so I bluffed my way by saying I felt so very nervous with the pressure of a new career riding on it, I'd rather not do it there and then, though to rest assured I was very good. I don't know how I got the job, but he took me on.

I successfully avoided typing any letters he wanted to dictate and instead told him it would be better if he recorded them all on tape and I'd get them taken care of – I did, but at the rate of about one a day. Maybe it was my chutzpah that saved me, but my boss seemed to like me and tolerated my obvious secretarial failings.

As our office dealt with many clients from Germany, France, Poland, Hungary and so forth, one day Mr Boublik informed me that many of the reps from those countries were coming in to meet him and that he would be hosting a cocktail party in their honour.

'Can you take care of mixing the drinks?' he asked, obviously thinking my talents might have lain in catering (as they certainly weren't in typing).

'Of course!' I exclaimed.

I was in my early 20s and barely drank, let alone had ever mixed a cocktail, but I wasn't going to admit that.

Boublik showed me the various bottles of vodka, cognac, gin, wine and so forth, and I nodded affirmatively. When the first rep arrived, he asked me for a whiskey. I took one of the lovely heavy glass tumblers and checked each label on the various bottles until I saw the one I was looking for and duly poured what I thought was a generous glug.

The rep looked at the glass, then at me, and in disbelief said, 'You're not supposed to pour it all the way to the top, just a tiny bit!'

'Oh, it saves me time on refills,' I laughed as I moved to greet the next rep to check what his tipple was.

Mr Boublik saw the funny side afterwards, but initially gave me a telling off, asking what sort of impression the reps were going to take away, but to be honest, he couldn't really keep a straight face. I guess he could have easily fired me at that point ... but no, he kept me on and a few months later even recommended me for a promotion to the accounts department – obviously the banking background listed on my CV had impressed him. Little did he know I was about as good with figures as I was with typing.

Working at Barrandov always seemed magical as I had grown up visiting the cinema regularly, and although my then husband worked in the sound department, it was very much in post-production and he never got to visit films on the stage floor. So, despite both he and I being present at the studios, we were quite distant from the heart of the action.

I actually spent three years working for Dermacol from 1973 until, one day, my dentist – who knew *everybody* – told me about a job vacancy with the big boss of the studio, Mr Jiří Hájek, who was in overall charge of all the productions at the studio. Thanks to my dentist, I secured an interview.

Hájek was a larger-than-life Czech man, who could be both extremely vulgar and rude but at the same time extremely kind-natured. I guess you had to get to know his character a little to know how to deal with him. We chatted and, of course, the fact I was based at Barrandov gave me a great 'in' with him as I knew the studio well and loved being there.

'I like you, and I think you'd be good in this job,' he said.

'But I can't type,' I said sheepishly, finally confessing to what I thought would be a major prerequisite for the role.

'That doesn't matter. I speak to people. I hardly ever write letters. Nobody reads them anyway,' he replied with a guffaw.

At that moment, I knew we'd get on, but added that I was working for Dermacol and would need to give notice if he wanted me.

'How much notice?'

I explained my contract had stated 'six months'.

'That's not possible, my secretary is leaving next week as she is pregnant and I need someone immediately,' he added.

My heart sank as he reached for the telephone, expecting him to ask his secretary to show me out, but no! He called my current boss and basically told him that I was leaving with immediate effect. The one side of the conversation I overheard went along the lines of, 'I don't care, she is leaving and starts with me next week.' End of call.

I was fortunately able to help find my own replacement, which smoothed things over slightly, but without doubt, this new job was the best move I'd ever made.

There would be up to twenty productions running at any one time, including a foreign production department (where I transferred to in 1981), and it was always tremendously busy and buzzing – though, of course, all state controlled at the end of the day.

Many hated Jiří Hájek because he was so forthright, and I often saw him look out of a window in his office only to spot a producer or other studio executive walking by, leap up and call them the most horrendously rude names and tell them how they were messing up on productions in the fruitiest of language. I think I'd met bricklayers with more cultured articulation.

But he got away with it as everyone accepted that was how he was. Nowadays, he'd probably be fired for bullying, but I have to admit that I liked him, and we got on very well. Whilst he didn't suffer fools gladly, I always made sure I was one step ahead of him and anticipated his next move, which he seemed to appreciate.

I think I worked on 52 films in my first year, mainly Czech, plus the odd Russian war film (a lot of propaganda), and an occasional foreign production. My office was in complete charge of all the extremely talented people and departments who, quite honestly, rivalled the best technicians and filmmakers in the West.

I can't say I was enamoured with the flag-waving subjects, which portrayed the communists and Russians as being the heroes in everything they touched. I remember one film about a nuclear power station that was leaking, and the potential ramifications, and anyone who remembers Chernobyl will know the scientists did not prevent disaster, but such was the outwardly portrayal of the glorified regime that the heroes were always Russian scientists who came to save the day.

If I'm honest, I much preferred the costume or fairytale type dramas and adventures we made, such as Cinderella or the Brothers Grimm stories, which proved very popular in cinemas. There was a total lack of any pictures from the West, apart from some twenty-year-old cowboy movies. State censors wouldn't allow modern films through, nor sanction any scripts which in any way portrayed Russians as anything but heroes.

Between 1976 and 1985, I progressed from being a general assistant (essentially making the tea and running errands as required), to production assistant, before becoming 'assistant to the head of production'. In developing my career, I also enrolled, between 1980 and 1984, at university one day a month at FAMU (The Film and TV School of the Academy of Performing Arts) in Prague, where I gained a Diploma Degree in Film & TV. This triggered my promotion to 'production manager', which was a much more responsible role across all aspects of a film, from budget, to schedule and crew, and reporting directly to the producers. People have asked me if the studios were like those in Britain and France, heavily unionised with tightly controlled working hours. Not really, as communism was a union in itself; we worked pretty civilised hours through until about 6pm and often six days a week when in production, though Saturdays were generally shorter days and Sundays were always free to spend with family. Overtime was rare – but then again, you were never paid even if you worked it!

We had a fairly decent canteen, and I remember one British producer describing it as having "greasy tables, greasy plastic tablecloths and grease on top of the soup – it was lovely"! Of course, there were dumplings with everything, which visitors quickly tired of.

In 1981, I transferred to the international production department at Barrandov. Western productions came to the country specifically for its castles, churches, and countryside – and with them they brought dollars, and Czechs wanted dollars, so they were very warmly welcomed – which is how I became assigned to Barbra Streisand to ensure everything ran smoothly during her stay. A little later, a British production designer named Peter Lamont came to recce for the James Bond film, *Octopussy*. Peter had been involved in the franchise since 1964 and was such a lovely man who appreciated my knowledge of the city and being able to open doors to the production. As it happens, the film shot in West Germany, but

Peter said I should be sure to look him up if I ever came to the UK or if I ever thought he could help with a production I was involved with. He meant it too – he was very sincere, and I held him to it when I needed to get my (later) partner, Frank, a job in England.

There was a moment when my new career in production coincided with my old one at Dermacol. You see, one of my perks of being in the international film department at Barrandov was that I got to visit the Karlovy Vary International Film Festival in the West Bohemian region of the country. The festival was founded in 1946 and has become Eastern Europe's leading film event.

Mr Hájek, who was in charge of my department, tried to avoid festivals but had to attend this (local) one as part of his job remit, and in 1980, he was actually invited to open the festival as guest of honour, which he seemed to hate even more.

He approached me and explained how he loathed festivals and particularly on his own, so he wondered if my colleague Alena and I would like to go along with him as his guests.

'Of course!' I exclaimed with immediate thoughts of the glamorous opening party, limousines, posh hotels and the like springing to mind. Not that I'm shallow, but any relief from the comparatively drab surroundings of Barrandov was very welcome.

We indeed attended the first night party and very much enjoyed ourselves with free-flowing champagne. At around 4am/5am, we started making our way back to the hotel – it was light by then in July – only to discover a massive cordon outside with police everywhere.

Being nosey, I approached a small group of onlookers to ask what was happening.

'You don't know?' one chap replied, as though I had been on another planet.

I shook my head.

'Well, a guy climbed up the front of the building, slipped and fell to his death.'

I felt a cold shudder down my spine at the thought of how awful an end to someone's life it was.

'Do you know who it was?' I asked, not really thinking it'd be anyone I'd heard of, let alone knew.

'Oh yes, he was the boss of Dermacol.'

My old company! My old boss! Mr Boublik!

The morning newspapers carried the story of how he had indeed climbed out of his room and had slipped, losing his footing whilst trying to reach another bedroom window.

It then all came out that Boublik had, in fact, been having a long-time affair with the founder of the company, Olga Knoblochová, who, together with Barrandov Film Studios, developed and manufactured the immensely successful and popular make-up brand. She was the most beautiful woman, who was divorced with two children. Boublik, on the other hand, was very much married with children. He had seemingly kept promising Olga that he'd divorce his wife, saying it was a loveless marriage, to be with her. Of course, he never did.

The affair was never spoken about within the company, but we all knew something was going on between them, and apparently, in the run-up to the film festival, she finally confronted him – it was either her or his wife.

But Boublik was a Catholic, and whilst he had certainly fallen for Olga, his religion meant divorce was out of the question.

Olga decided to end the relationship and said she wanted nothing more to do with him. With that, she left Prague for Karlovy Vary in order to put some space between them... but Boublik followed her.

Olga was a regular at the festival as, of course, the make-up was *the* preferred choice in Hollywood circles, and she took her regular suite at the hotel. She instructed the front of house security not to let anyone up to her room, particularly her jilted beau.

However, the amorous Boublik refused to take no for an answer and with it being a hot summer evening, he noticed the window in Olga's suite was open, so he shouted up from the pavement, 'Olga, Olga, we have to talk...'

She ignored him, which led him to scale the outside of the building... and fall.

I recently read that Boublik's daughter has now, four decades on, stated he was not having an affair nor trying to reach Olga, but rather was attending the festival only to find himself locked and trapped inside his own hotel room. He then, allegedly, attempted to get out through the window...

There are those doubters who believe she may be looking at her father's life through rose-tinted glasses all these years on. I couldn't possibly comment.

***

My husband Tony was, at heart, a sincere and hardworking man employed in the sound department at Barrandov. Soon after we married, we became friends with a couple, Luděk and Vlasta Konhoffer, with whom we shared similar interests, and they too had a son – about 9 or 10 – so we always enjoyed spending time socially with them, as in a way I guess we looked up to them having raised a young boy of their own. Luděk worked at Barrandov with my husband but was quite often taken away on location for film work.

The wife, Vlasta, was maybe ten years older than us, at around 35, and was very attractive. Very, very attractive in fact. I now realise how naïve I was, but it took me a while to discover my husband had fallen for this woman.

After Martin was born, my husband became the sole breadwinner for the house whilst I cared for our sickly child, and he seemed to be working longer and longer days with the excuse of needing to bring extra money in; that all made perfect sense, of course, and I never for one minute questioned him. Vlasta phoned occasionally and nearly always with the pretence of needing to ask my husband his advice about something or other. He'd usually raise his eyebrows to me as if to say, 'Oh, not her again,' and I'd busy myself around the apartment whilst they chatted. It was always something mundane, or at least he said it was, and as Vlasta's husband wasn't very good with practical things and was often away with his work, it all seemed plausible.

One particular evening, we had just finished eating dinner – on a rare occasion, my husband had come home early – when the telephone rang, and again it was Vlasta. This time, it was with the excuse of her boiler having broken down, meaning she had no hot water, so she asked if he would go over right away.

'Of course!' he said, as he grabbed his coat.

'You must be joking!' I exclaimed, telling him this was an opportunity for us to spend an evening together for the first time in weeks, yet he reasoned he must go to Vlasta's aid?!

He went and didn't return home until 1am, and he reeked of Vlasta's perfume. It was then that I knew something was going on.

I started thinking back to the phone calls, the late returns home and all of the 'advice' Vlasta was continually asking for. I rummaged around for my husband's salary paperwork and our savings book and saw there was no extra money coming in for all of his so-called overtime.

I froze.

My life as I knew it was unravelling, and the man I trusted and loved most had clearly deceived me.

At work, I always remained calm in a crisis, and decided I needed to be just as calm here. I said nothing, and instead waited for the next evening he was (supposedly) working late and waited for him. When he eventually walked in, he again reeked of that same perfume.

I confronted him with the facts and accused him of having an affair. He stood staring at me, unable to deny anything.

I needed to get some air; I needed to think, and despite the late hour, I went to see my mom and tell her what had happened.

'What are you going to do?' she asked.

Martin was not even one year old at that point.

'I'm not sure, but I cannot be with him anymore – that I do know,' I replied.

My husband was flattered, turned on and excited in equal measure by this vivacious older woman who found him so desirable. She, in turn, had played him very well to get exactly what she wanted – she was certainly no innocent!

'I will help you and support you,' my mother said, 'but you need to find a solicitor and divorce him.'

I thought about it all overnight and the next morning said, 'No, mum. I don't want Martin to grow up without a father. I don't want him to come from a broken home. Things will be on my terms and on my conditions going forward.

'He has to stop seeing her, we will live in the same apartment but not as a couple, and I will only divorce him when Martin understands,' I added.

We co-habited but were very much living separate lives. I went through a whole rollercoaster of emotions, but the one thing that kept eating away at me more than any other was anger – I wanted my husband to feel the pain of betrayal that I had felt.

I admit I had several one-night stands and met several men, probably thinking I was getting my own back and hurting him. Though, if anything, it probably just added to my own hurt and wasn't the solution at all. I guess I felt I was empowering myself and taking control, for a short while at least, and it felt good to reverse the tables on him and to let him know I was out having 'fun'.

As Martin grew up and adapted to the household situation, I don't believe he ever knew, at least I don't think, about the total charade we were living. Or did he?

My husband and I were always civilised and never argued in front of Martin, who was the innocent party after all. We rarely went out together as a couple unless it was to a work function where we were expected to be there, for example, as husband and wife, but it was all for show. There was no trust between us, and certainly not a chance of reconciliation. Our holidays were spent separately, and conversation was mainly about household matters. When Martin turned 13, I felt it was time to talk to him about our living arrangements. I've always said he was wise beyond his years, as he said he completely understood, which in turn allowed me to say, 'OK, now it's time to sort a divorce.' I was also beginning to plan my escape, so I wanted all loose ends tied up.

All these years later, I'm actually now friends with my ex-husband, who has married again – for the third time – and in fact I'm good friends with his wife too. It's strange how things work out sometimes, isn't it?

When he reached 18, Martin asked me if I minded him contacting his father, who he hadn't really seen or communicated with since our divorce five years earlier – and of course I said he should, as when all was said and done, they are father and son. They now have a good relationship, so I'm pleased.

CHAPTER 3

Escape – Part One

At the time of Barbra Streisand's arrival in Prague, I was going through my divorce, and Martin and I had now moved out of the family apartment to my mother's.

I had successfully managed to hide my growing hatred of Soviet rule and oppression, and always did my job to the best of my ability, and never, ever let on to anyone that I was even thinking about the slightest possibility of a life outside our communist ideal.

But it was Barbra who became the catalyst for triggering my life change.

Being in the film industry for several years by that point, I had learned the importance of planning and preparation – time spent on preparation was seldom ever wasted – and Barbra was of a similar mindset, paying attention to every little detail.

She had secured the screen rights to 'Yentl' in 1969, with the intention of starring in the title role, but feeling she was too old (she was then in her late 20s), one by one, potential directors and producers decided her casting would prove too much of a distraction. Never one to give up, and after completing *A Star Is Born* in 1976, for which she won her second Oscar, Barbra was convinced she wasn't too old to play the lead and, furthermore, decided she would also direct. Despite her Academy-Award winning status, studio paymasters were fearful of a first-time director and particularly one who also wanted to star in a multi-million-dollar proposition. In the end, all the majors deemed it too much of a gamble and declined to become involved.

A couple of years later, in 1978, the story was re-imagined as a musical, in the hope it might be more commercial (riding on the popularity of *Grease*), but Barbra's partner Jon Peters instead tried to persuade her to perform at Wembley Stadium in London, for a tantalising offer of $1 million. Barbra refused. She also refused a second offer of $2 million! She even refused a third offer, said to be in excess of $10 million, to perform in Las Vegas – she simply wanted to make *Yentl*.

With the continued rejections, even Jon Peters began to think the studio doubters had a point about her age and her playing a male character. He changed his mind when one night a strange man broke into the house and, upon confronting the burglar, Barbra revealed it was her in full make-up and costume. Duly convinced of her ability to play a man, Peters was able to negotiate a deal with new studio, Orion Pictures, on the condition that Yentl's age was changed from 16 to 26. An announcement about the film was made in the summer of 1980, soon after which Barbra travelled to Prague with a Super-8 camera and song lyrics to scout out film locations. However, no sooner had Barbra got back to LA than *Heaven's Gate* (1980), a Michael Cimino picture produced by United Artists lost $35 million at the box office – an unprecedented amount – which effectively brought the studio to its knees and prompted a nervous Orion (along with most other studios) to cancel all films budgeted over $10 million.

Yentl was priced at $14 million and was put into turnaround – in film language, that means cancelled and put up for sale.

The project was subsequently turned down again and again by other equally nervous financiers until Jon Peters, Peter Gruber, and Neil Bogart formed PolyGram Pictures, secured a line of credit from banks and agreed to back *Yentl* themselves.

However, with four strong characters, creative differences arose, and coupled with personal disputes between Streisand and Peters, resulting in their relationship ending, it all meant *Yentl* was dropped yet again.

Fifteen years after its original conception and 20 script drafts later, *Yentl's* production finally began with backing from United Artists (which had merged with MGM) under the new leadership of Freddie Fields and David Begelman, Barbra

Streisand's former agent from the late 1960s. Budgeted at $14.5 million, the film went $1.5 million over, which Barbra paid for personally. I, alas, was not allowed to rejoin the production in Prague by my employers, because they had by then become suspicious about me and dispatched me northwards to work on a Russian film.

Throughout her visit, Barbra kept telling me, 'You are wasted here, Lidia, you really are wasted – you should come to America to work.'

She opened my eyes to the possibility of a life and career outside of the regime I detested so much.

I should add that when Barbra was out and about on recces, she'd always book a restaurant to host her entire accompanying team. One lunchtime, she invited me to join them all, and just as we settled into our chairs, she looked around and asked, 'Where are all the drivers?'

They were, in fact, in another room in the building, but Barbra insisted they were just as important to the production as all the cast and crew were, and insisted they join us – and from that point on should always eat with us. Barbra was always very thoughtful and generous in that way.

On another such evening, she hosted a dinner in the most expensive restaurant in Prague, with beautiful crystal chandeliers, wonderful glassware and solid silver cutlery... it was total opulence. There was, however, very little in the way of food. After all, it was a communist state and there wasn't much indulgence offered on the menus!

Among the guests – though not necessarily involved with *Yentl* – were several Westerners, including production designer Peter Lamont and Warner Bros. head of international production Paul Hitchcock. I was sitting next to my Czech colleague when Paul came over and said to her, 'Would you mind moving to another seat as I'd like to sit here?'

Knowing who Paul was, my colleague quietly moved.

Oh my god! This is the head of a major US studio, and I'm representing the Czech film industry to him. He'll think I'm the village idiot! I thought to myself ahead of smiling, nodding and saying 'Yes' to almost everything he said without really understanding what any of the conversation was about – aside from catching a handful of words from the interpreter on the other side of the table who was translating some of Paul's conversation to a few of the other gathered executives.

Paul was very charming and a total gentleman, so I was rather taken aback when he wrote something on a napkin and slipped it into my hand. I looked down to see, 'I love you.'

Okay, we've known each other for two hours, I can hardly communicate in his language, let alone impress him with wit and intelligence, and he loves me?! I thought. I glanced quizzically at what he was drinking, smiled politely and said nothing more.

Years later, when we met again, Paul confirmed, 'I really meant it!'

It sounds a little crazy (especially to sensible old me) but then again, you do hear stories about love at first sight, and I recall Michael Caine saying he spotted Shakira in a coffee commercial one evening and became instantly besotted by her beauty and radiance; so much so, he declared, 'I'm going to marry that woman.' And he did.

Anyhow, Paul left his office number and said the usual, 'If there's anything I can ever help you with…'

(I did take him up on his offer when my son Martin decided he wanted to work in the film industry some years later in London and needed some work experience ahead of going to university. Paul – true to his promise – invited him to help catalogue and pack up the Warner Soho office for a move out to Pinewood Studios, where a new bungalow had been built for the company. But I'm getting ahead of myself here…)

***

With plans set for Barbra's return to Prague to commence filming in a matter of months, I enrolled in English classes and hoped the offer to join her in Hollywood afterwards was genuine.

But the Czech authorities' suspicions of me grew when an established American producer named Larry DeWaay came to Prague for a short time to investigate setting up a film – which I don't think was ever made in the end – and left behind an envelope for me.

I was called into the producer's office where he presented me with it, saying he had no idea what it contained, but of course, he knew as he'd already opened it! To my great surprise, there was a lovely note saying 'Thank you, you have been wonderful, and I appreciate all you've done to help' along with $100.

The look of contempt on the producer's face remains with me today, and Larry had unwittingly put me in a difficult position. It appeared I had been befriending Westerners, though the fact I was just doing my job, and doing it well, was neither here nor there – it was as though I had shown my disrespect to the communist party.

From that point on, the studio held me back to work only on Czech and Russian productions.

***

The international film department at Barrandov always involved 'Film Export' as their (local) co-production company, which consisted mainly of staff cooperating with the ŠtB. The company employed drivers of the most luxurious Russian limousines, which were all placed at the disposal of foreign film-makers – they too were all ŠtB collaborators.

I remember American director Richard Donner visiting and saying he was so impressed with the cars that he wanted to buy one to be shipped out to LA, but Film Export said it was 'impossible'. Of course it was, as they didn't want anyone to realise the cars were stuffed full of listening devices. The bugs, along with the charming drivers, ensured every conversation that took place on the back seat was monitored.

Thank goodness I was never a passenger in one of those cars, but I did foolishly mention to one of the drivers – you see how green and innocent I was – that I thought the Austrian producer he was driving around was very attractive and how I had a bit of a crush on him, not realising this was all being fed back to the ŠtB. Luckily, that's all I ever said.

***

It was so important that each step of my plan seemed natural and didn't raise any suspicion of unusual behaviour, nor did I do anything too out of my ordinary routine, but goodness, when I look back, I realise there were so many little things that could have gone wrong.

I never told my mother any details of my plan, partly for her own safety but also because if a single word of it ever came out, then I knew I would be thrown into prison for the rest of my life and never see Martin or my mum again. The stakes were high, but so was the prize – freedom.

Despite having passports, travel was very restricted outside of the country to the West, where family members were only ever allowed to journey alone – my son was able to go abroad, for example, as was I, but we could never travel together, even for a holiday.

The authorities were (rightly) fearful that families simply wouldn't come back, and by ensuring some members were 'left behind', it guaranteed a return.

At all times, I had to think one step ahead of the bureaucrats, the police and the so-called Home Office (or Secret Police as we knew them better). So, in 1984, a year before our escape, I sent my teenage son on an educational school trip to Austria with a good friend of mine from the studio, Frank, looking after him – as a sort of guardian figure. I wanted to establish Martin on a pattern of travelling, firstly to prove to the authorities he would obey all the rules and return and was not a flight risk; and secondly, because Martin had never left Czechoslovakia in his life and I needed him to build his confidence a little and experience the culture of another country. I didn't want Martin to feel too scared or be too daunted, as he only spoke Czech, though children, I have learned, are very adaptable and can be quite fearless. Thank goodness.

Unlike Martin, I knew Frank wouldn't be returning home from the trip, as he saw it as his chance to get away to the West. Travelling as a responsible adult with Martin was seen as a safe bet in the eyes of the Secret Police, and the fact that Martin returned (despite Frank flitting) also proved to the authorities that he and I were a law-abiding family. We both feigned shock upon hearing Frank had absconded, which all helped strengthen our standing as good comrades.

Carefully and quietly, I helped arrange some introductions for Frank through production designer Peter Lamont and with contacts I'd made in the Austrian film industry, in particular a script supervisor who had worked in Prague and with whom I'd become quite friendly; she helped Frank get to a displacement camp, where he claimed political asylum. With his skills as an art director, he said he wanted to settle in London, and although it took him a few months to be 'processed', Frank eventually arrived in the UK – and that is exactly where I needed him to be. It was all part of my plan.

I could, of course, have tried to get to the USA, where I knew Barbra Streisand would have offered me a job and where my old boyfriend Oli (who escaped in late 1968) lived. But the thought of being so very far away from my mother was one I simply could not bear, even though it was unlikely I'd ever be allowed back to Prague. Being in Europe at least meant I felt closer to Mum. I hoped there might one day be a chance we could reunite – never imagining that Communism would fall, of course!

***

My late father had always dreamed about owning a restaurant and, with the slightest encouragement, would go into great detail about how he envisioned it; the type of clientele he'd host, the food he would serve and so on. He painted a wonderful picture of a meeting place, a hub of great conversation, centred around the very best food and wine. But alas, entrepreneurialism wasn't encouraged in communist countries, and after the war, the nearest he got was when he worked in a high-end restaurant in Prague. I'd regularly visit him on Fridays, after classes, as I was such a miserable eater in school that my big treat of the week was to pig out on schnitzel and potato salad in a booth. I'd refuel for the week ahead and receive the very best service, of course.

Sunday was a family day, and so Dad didn't work but made a point of the family being together at home for lunch each week at our apartment in Prague 5, on the embankment of the Vltava river. Afterwards, he and I would go on a big walk through the city and end up in a café where he would read the newspaper over a coffee while I demolished an ice cream sundae. He was always keen that he and I spent that time together, plus he knew it gave mum a break.

Despite my father's warm, fun, outgoing nature, there was something that lay beneath, an unhappiness, a bitterness. His parents had been farmers, with land and livestock, but that all disappeared when the communists took control. My grandparents stood, broken people, with nothing left, and my father never forgave the regime.

Dad was a tall, slim and fit man, but through his later years, he was plagued with heart problems, all culminating in one final fatal heart attack. There's no doubt in my mind that his untimely death was due to the unhappiness and bitterness that festered inside, eating away at him like a cancer.

I felt very angry after his death. For at least 6 months, I was disruptive, tearful and sad. In fact, I was so consumed in my own grief that I never really thought my poor mum was just as tearful and angry; she was widowed at 42 and landed with an angry teenager too.

Fortunately, I turned a corner and 'grew up'.

Then came marriage and Martin, and a determination to give my son a better life – a life away from Czechoslovakia. The seeds were obviously sown early on in my mind.

When I talk of 'escape', it may perhaps sound a little dramatic, but Czechoslovakia was a country literally fenced in, sometimes electrified fences, leading to many people losing their lives trying to get through.

It wasn't quite the Berlin Wall penning us in, but it wasn't that much different, I assure you.

CHAPTER 4

Escape – Part Two

I carried on with my work at Barrandov, and Martin settled back into school and his everyday routine. Though the authorities initially questioned us about Frank, they pretty much left us alone when they realised we were honestly quite clueless as to where he was.

Though I dared not try to contact him directly for fear of giving him away or implicating myself in his absconding, shortly afterwards, I did hear through my contacts that all was ok, and he had reached London and secured work in the film industry. Most vital of all, he was 'in place' for me as I very much needed him to be my contact and to make arrangements for our own arrival.

In the same corridor as my office at Barrandov was a little room with a husband-and-wife team who ran the 'Personnel Office'. She was quite pleasant, but he was rather vicious – and whenever any studio staff left the country to work on a film, they would be interviewed beforehand by this couple and then again after returning. Perhaps 'interrogated' would be a better description rather than 'interviewed'. The 'personnel officers' were, of course, ŠtB and all closely associated with the KGB. I'm sure they monitored our phone lines, and I later discovered all our offices were bugged, so we were certainly monitored from every angle and had to be extremely careful about what we said and who we trusted.

I knew I couldn't travel with my son Martin anywhere out of the country, so I needed to find two trips to two very different areas, but which coincided – I would go on one, whilst he would go on the other in the opposite direction. Far enough apart so as to not arouse suspicion, but close enough to put us within touching distance of one another.

Ahead of this, and in order to gain a new passport, I took on a Czechoslovak Holocaust movie made in Krakow, Poland called *Zastihla me noc* (*Caught by Night*) directed by Juraj Herz, which I also thought would be useful to have on my resume to show I had production experience outside of Prague, as I hoped to get film work in London just as Frank had and I knew how important varied credits would be. It was a deeply traumatic storyline and gave me nightmares for years, about the slow death of communist journalist and Prague City Council member Jozka Jaburková in the Ravensbrück concentration camp. It was only later that I discovered the director, Juraj Herz, was imprisoned in the same camp as a child – he didn't make another movie for over 20 years, such was its effect on him.

During post-production (back in Prague), I was at the music recording studio when one of my assistants came in to tell me there were two men outside who wanted to speak with me. I said he should tell them that the session finished at 6pm, and I could not possibly leave until then.

Within a minute, the assistant returned and said, 'Lidia, you have to come out, *now*.'

I knew immediately when I saw the two plainclothes policemen standing there that I had a problem.

'Do you have your passport on you?' they asked.

I sort of laughed and said, 'Why would I have my passport at a music session?'

'Where is your passport?' they snapped.

'It's at home,' I answered dutifully.

'Then you come with us there now,' they replied.

'May I ask what this is about?' I enquired.

'You don't ask questions; you just come with us now and give us your passport!'

I left with them, but all the way home tried to figure out what was going on and made innocent remarks about being busy with the film and that sort of thing – basically trying to appear slightly annoyed at the inconvenience of it all.

One of the two policemen looked at me squarely in the eye and said, 'We have reports you are planning to escape.'

I laughed and said they must be crazy. I had a wonderful job, my dream job in fact, a wonderful family and a wonderful life in Prague. Why on earth would I want to go anywhere else?

Of course, it was all bullshit, and they didn't buy any of it.

I handed my passport to them and realised I'd now be on their watch list. I was absolutely devastated – I'd spent over a year planning so far and had failed.

The next day, I had to report to the Secret Police office in Prague, which is a very dominating and oppressive-looking building. I was ushered into a room which contained a basic table and two chairs. I waited, and waited, until after two hours, a man appeared and asked if I knew why I was there. I said, 'No.'

'There has been a report to Barrandov Studios that you are planning an escape,' he said and mentioned Frank's name, suggesting I had a part in his disappearance. I looked terrified – quite genuinely – and protested that I hardly knew Frank, he was just someone I had worked with and somebody at the studio must have been feeding bullshit stories about me, as they were probably jealous of my success.

The man stared at me, emotionless.

I then told him how Martin had been on a trip to Austria and had returned home, and that we were both good law-abiding comrades and I would never do anything against the party. I should have won an acting award!

It seems the ŠtB discovered Frank had arrived in London, and after a little further digging, figured out that he and I had been good friends, and in fact we became romantically involved for a short time ahead of his escape, so of course assumed I'd try to join him there. (We did live together in London later on, but whilst I was happy for us just to be good friends, Frank felt it should be something more, which put a strain on our friendship – I'll come to that later).

I was in that room until 6pm without any drink or food, and there was even a change of shift when my interrogator went home, only for another to arrive and start all over. I continued to protest my innocence throughout.

'You have two options now,' he stated finally at the end of the day, 'to either admit your guilt, or to prove what you are saying is true and prove your loyalty.'

He then changed tact. 'We know your immediate boss, Helen, in the Western production office, has a brother who escaped, and we know she is talking to him – we want to know what he is saying and where he is.'

They wanted me to spy for them. That was the moment I realised our offices must have been bugged for them to know about Helen's calls.

I explained I couldn't question my superior about her brother – it was simply not the done thing and would immediately arouse her suspicion.

'You will be our eyes and ears, and when she calls him, you need to make sure she uses a certain telephone.'

'But how can I?' I asked. 'We're not even friends, we're just colleagues.'

'You just make sure. Each month we will meet, and you will report back.'

'How will we meet?' I asked, thankful that they were not so interested in me but rather in what I could find out for them. 'I will make arrangements,' he replied before nodding at the door for me to leave.

The next day, I went to work at Barrandov as usual and approached my boss, Helen and quietly asked her to come outside with me. She declined. When she next went to the bathroom, I followed her and said, 'Helen, I need to tell you something…'

'What?'

'They know about you and your brother, and they want you to use a particular phone when you call him next.'

She looked at me for a moment and simply said, 'OK. We will just talk about the weather.'

That's exactly what she did, and a month later, when I met my ŠtB contact, he asked, 'What is new?'

'I persuaded her to use the phone like you asked.'

'How did you do that?' he queried.

'I came up with some bullshit about needing to keep lines free for American producers and just to use that one phone for other calls. I can come up with excuses!'

'But so far we have nothing from her!' he exclaimed.

'Look, I did what you asked, and she is using that phone, but I can't make her talk,' I replied.

'I hope next month you will have something...'

Four weeks later, we met again, and again he said they still had nothing and that he would take me back to the secret police headquarters if I didn't cooperate.

'How can I make her talk?!' I asked briskly.

'Trigger something!'

I knew I'd never get Helen to say anything incriminating that would place either her or her brother in danger, so I needed to do something. But what?

My secret police handler was relatively young, probably late 30s or 40s, quite handsome and had he not been secret police, I imagined he would have actually been quite interesting company. So, I took a gamble.

'You know something...?' I asked him after a few meetings.

'What?'

'You are a very good-looking man...' I added, in my best flirty manner, though not knowing which way it might all go.

He smiled.

I'm not proud of myself, but we ended up in bed together that night and that was the last time I saw him. You see, the ŠtB realised their agent was compromised. Their spy had been seduced and could no longer be trusted, so he was recalled.

I had thought maybe he'd be a little less persistent in pressing me for information if I turned the tables on him, but my gamble had paid off infinitely better – I was now free of them. Talk about sleeping with the enemy.

Whilst they weren't actively following me, I was obviously marked as being a 'non-communist person' and we found things started to become a little more difficult in everyday life. My son at school, for example, was sidelined by his teachers for certain classes and activities. Martin had his whole future ahead of him, but it was becoming obvious he would never be allowed to achieve his full potential. Added to this, I was being sidelined from films I should have been working on – the 'personnel office' (aka the secret police) down the corridor saw to that and had me relegated to cheap, boring Russian propaganda movies.

All this further confirmed my belief that, aged 37, I needed to get away sooner rather than later. I could see the future, and it wasn't going to be good for us, so if ever I needed reassurance I was doing the right thing, this was it.

I was actually at a good age – mature enough to know how the minds of the authoritarians worked and how to best plan every eventuality, but also young and energetic enough to adapt to a new life, a new language and a new culture.

I had a good working relationship with the General Manager of Barrandov Studios, Dr Fabera. Outwardly, he was pro-communist – and had to be seen to be – but I felt he wasn't quite so enthusiastic in private. He was highly intelligent, spoke several languages, wrote books, and was academically very exceptional – all the things communists hated. When I saw things were not going to plan, I asked him if we could meet, and said it was about 'private matters'. He gave me his home number and told me to call him there, obviously knowing his phone at the studio was bugged. I did so, and he suggested the following Saturday we should meet at a local cemetery – a very interesting choice of meeting place, I thought.

'I have a feeling you have something very secretive to discuss,' Fabera said when he saw my slightly puzzled face as I walked between the tombstones towards him.

I told him how I had been interrogated, threatened about my job and how my son's life was now being affected. I asked him what I should do for the best? I didn't mention the word 'escape' – yes, I trusted him, but not totally.

'Lidia, you need to leave the studio. You will never be allowed to progress – you will go from bad films to worse films and end up resenting your career,' he suggested.

'But that's my whole life, my income,' I replied, knowing I still had a year to go of planning my escape.

'You asked for my advice – leave,' he added.

'But I need a reason! I love the business, and I've progressed from assistant to production manager. Why would I give it all up suddenly?' I asked, thinking how it would look to outsiders.

'You'll find a way,' Fabera replied with a little smile.

If I was going to resign and not arouse suspicion, then I needed to plant ideas. Being divorced, I figured the suggestion of me having met a man would sound completely plausible, and so I began developing a story about a new man in my life. He was highly intelligent, had a good job, but lived outside of Prague in Moravia. I said we had been swept along in a whirlwind love affair and we were discussing marriage. All rubbish, of course, but I made it sound convincing.

I developed my charade over several weeks and even visited a printer shop where I had wedding invitations, complete with a date, venue address, etc. made for the following summer. I distributed these cards to colleagues at the studio and explained I was soon going to move to be with my love and sadly would be giving my notice, but that I wanted them to all be part of our special day when it arrived. The invitations featured the name of my bridegroom, who was in fact a man I met once on a train. He sat opposite me and, as we chatted to pass the time, he introduced himself. He told me he was heading home to a town in the north. So, in using his name and hometown, I thought if anyone should look him up, they'd at least see he was real – I just hoped they didn't then talk to him about his upcoming nuptials!

I never told my mum any of this, by the way, I explained that I was between films so wouldn't be at the studio as much. Though after a few weeks, she asked, 'How come you are home *so* much?'

I came up with excuses about how we'd been doing recces for films, and I didn't have to go back to the office as frequently until production started. She knew I wasn't telling the truth but never asked any more.

By this point, I had less than a year to go before my final trip and made sure that I bored everyone with details about my upcoming wedding. Meanwhile, I eked out my savings and it actually gave me much more free time to plan for every eventuality. I then hid the remaining few invitations under my bed.

I've already mentioned that I couldn't travel on my own to any capitalist country, but I was allowed to travel as part of an organised group tour – and there were regular cultural trips to cities, including London, that I could book.

However, I didn't have a passport! I needed to find a way of getting a new one. But how?

Then the idea hit me. 'Mum, will you be travelling anywhere this year?' I asked.

'No, why?' she replied.

'So, you won't need your passport...?'

I had over a year to go but knew without the document it was pointless even trying to proceed with plans. My mother didn't ask any questions; she just handed me her passport.

Our surnames and addresses were the same (after I divorced, I reverted to my maiden name), but birthdays and photographs were different. 'Well, Mum, I heard that if you accidentally wash a passport in a trouser pocket, certain parts of it fade and disappear.'

We washed that passport twice! Indeed, the photograph faded nicely, the date of birth all but disappeared and you could just about make out the address.

I made an appointment to visit the passport office, not quite knowing whether they'd have a big black mark against my name or not.

'Look at this, how stupid am I, I forgot my passport was in my pocket and washed it...' I said pitifully as I presented the dog-eared paperwork.

'How could you be so careless? And so stupid!' the clerk snapped.

I cowered sheepishly and took the dressing down she delivered.

'Do you have any ID?' she asked.

I took out my birth certificate and details of my address, shaking all the time as I knew if the secret police discovered what I was doing, I'd be imprisoned for life.

The clerk looked it all over, whilst still tutting at me, and copied down all the details.

'We will notify you when it is ready. It should be about three weeks until your new one is issued,' she added sharply.

I thanked her and quietly left the office. Sure enough, a few weeks later, a shiny new passport arrived. The plan was back on.

I started going over everything with Martin: what he would have to do, where he would have to go, and that whilst I would give him some money, he wasn't to show it or talk about it with anyone. I explained how he would meet up with me again and, hopefully, begin our new lives – I went through every little aspect of the plan over and over with him for weeks and months, and kept emphasising that he must not breathe a word of it to another living soul. There could be no room for error.

Rolling forward, I booked Martin on a coach tour to Italy, travelling through Germany and France, with lots of other schoolchildren of his age. It was headed by two tour guides, one of whom was almost certainly a secret police officer, and I stressed to Martin that he wouldn't know which one of the two was ŠtB, so he shouldn't trust either, even with the most casual of comments.

The final stop of his trip was to be Venice.

I meanwhile booked myself a Communist-group sightseeing tour to London, departing after Martin but arriving in the capital five days before Martin was due to leave Italy.

I told my mother we were planning to leave on separate trips and would probably not see her again for some time, so she knew but wasn't aware of the finer details.

She took Martin to the coach station to meet his excursion whilst I stayed home, nervously pottering around trying to keep myself busy and watching the clock tick.

At 10am, my mother returned and nodded. Martin was underway, and I breathed a huge sigh of relief, that is, until I noticed the hall table where he had left the bundle of money and a piece of paper with some UK contacts I had given to him! Okay, he had a little pocket money, but not enough to pay for taxis and food after he 'disappeared' from his group. My heart sank.

Although Martin was by then just 15 years of age, he was very mature and knew our plan off by heart, and my instinct told me I should still go ahead with my trip, feeling he'd surely find a way through.

***

About a month before my own departure, I had started to pack; I was only able to take one small bag, and of course, as it was summer, I was careful to choose light clothes, as packing any winter ones would be difficult to explain if my case was checked. I couldn't risk taking any documents such as birth certificates for either me or my son, nor a divorce certificate, family photographs and so on either, as that'd surely give me away on what was supposed to be a short trip to see London's highlights. But I knew I would need my precious documents and some personal possessions to join me, so in the last weeks before I left, I set aside three suitcases, but how would I be reunited with them?

Frank had put me in touch with a Major who had previously served in the Secret Police – Frank had done some improvement work on the guy's house – and assured me he was 'one of the good ones' and could help. I didn't know anything about this Major or whether he could be trusted, but Frank assured me that he could be… for a price. If I'd learned anything about communist life, it was that anybody could be bought for the right price, and all political affiliations were swiftly dropped!

The Major met me a week before my planned departure, took the suitcases (and payment) and told me they would be cared for by some very close friends of his in East Germany, near the border, until I was settled. He gave me their name and address and furthermore told me that when I departed for London, he would accompany me to the airport to ensure I got away okay, which was very reassuring.

But then he added, 'IF the police should come, you don't know me, and I don't know you!'

Had I not been worried before, I certainly was now. I kept hearing those words, 'IF the police should come…' over and over in my mind for the rest of the week, and I lost so much weight; it was better than any diet I've ever tried, though I wouldn't recommend that all-consuming feeling of stress and anxiety to anyone.

Picking up on my increasing anxiety, my mother said she couldn't be at the house, so she went to stay with her sister; to be honest, I felt better that she wasn't around, as I didn't want to implicate her in any way, and she'd have probably ended up stressing more than me.

The Major promised he'd keep an eye on me from the plane viewing area of the airport terminal and added, 'I will hopefully see your flight take off.'

Hopefully?! What did he mean, hopefully?

I was literally sick, worried that if the authorities had found out, they wouldn't let me get near the plane, and I had visions of being arrested at the boarding gate.

That fateful morning, I tried to compose myself and locked up the apartment, never knowing if I'd ever see our home again, before heading for the airport. I checked in with the tour group, trying to smile and look excited, whereas in fact I had begun shaking and trembling, as a sense of panic set in, rendering me almost motionless and speechless as I approached the security screening area. With my brain in a haze, I suddenly realised I had stuffed all the money I had saved – to support us for six months – into everything from underwear and shoes to pockets, socks and blouses. I also had some cash in my purse, just enough for my expenses, but it struck me that if the airport security people opened up my case and took my clothes out, they'd have surely found the cash. But the people in the queue behind me kept shuffling forward, and so I just moved along, and thankfully, the monotony of seeing lines of excited Czech tourists going away meant the staff didn't really worry about what any particular single person was taking out of the country.

I dared not show the slightest flicker of worry, so with my best straight face, I moved through security to the departure gate area where I took a seat, all the time trying not to look people walking by in the eye for fear of giving myself away. I may have given the appearance of a seasoned traveller, but inside my stomach was turning over and my heart was pounding as if it might burst out of my chest at any moment.

I never saw the Major, whether he was there or not, but kept saying to myself, if I can just board calmly and wait for the door to close on the plane, then I'd be home free – and I had to focus on that end result. Boarding was called, and the adrenaline kicked in. I moved with the group to my seat, where I tightened the safety belt and grabbed onto the armrests, as if for dear life. The stewardess gave me a warm smile, probably thinking I was a nervous flyer, and I wasn't about to tell her otherwise. My heart pounded louder, my breathing became faster until… the door closed, and we taxied to the runway.

***

On July 8th, 1985, I landed at Heathrow Airport. It was much the same as any other airport, really, except perhaps busier, and from the arrivals hall we all boarded a coach to central London and our hotel. The thing that struck me on the drive in was the advertising billboards, promoting all sorts of colourful things from cars and holidays to cigarettes. We never had those in Prague – yes, there were sometimes posters, but they were usually with a soldier holding a Soviet flag.

The cars seemed grander and bigger in London than back home, and there were, of course, black cabs and red buses which I'd seen photos of, all buzzing about and weaving through the bustling streets. And the shops! Of course, we had big stores in Prague, but the window displays were sparse and depressing, whilst in London they were full of products and excitement. It was as though a wonderful, warm colour filter had been dropped in front of my eyes after years of seeing everything in dull and drab light.

My tour group was led by two guides – one of whom was ŠtB – and we all stayed in the same 2-star London hotel, where we all went down for meals at the same time and all left on excursions together, so it was tightly controlled in that respect, and we were kept under watchful eyes at all times.

The next morning, I slipped down to reception via the back stairs of the hotel with my little bag and spotted Frank and a friend who were pretending to be tourists, looking at leaflets about London museums and such like. I was due to board a tourist coach with my group, and I knew I wouldn't be able to return to my belongings afterwards, so I needed Frank to take them. Like in a scene reminiscent of an old spy movie, I placed my suitcase down whilst looking at the same leaflets, and Frank picked it up before walking into the busy street outside. We said nothing, nor did we acknowledge one another.

It was the first time I'd been to London, so I was quite keen to see the sights, and after all, I was using the bus trip as a cover to make my escape. When we pulled into Parliament Square and marvelled at the Palace of Westminster and Big Ben – buildings we'd only seen in pictures and films – I pulled out my camera and started snapping photos like an over-enthusiastic sightseer and pointed out Westminster Abbey on the opposite side of the square. We were not allowed to leave the bus, but when the driver innocently pulled up outside the Abbey, I whipped the whole group into an excited frenzy about getting some photographs – and we were all allowed to disembark. I don't think the driver really appreciated that he was giving me the chance I needed, and after stepping off the coach, I slipped into the crowd of tourists, melding with and being absorbed by them.

I left a note on my seat: 'Don't wait for me, I am staying in this country. Lidia Lukes'

I moved very quickly and very carefully across London to a pre-arranged meeting place with Frank, where we disappeared into the London Underground and changed a couple of times to different tube trains to fully ensure no one was following.

'Why did you leave a note?' Frank asked me, somewhat puzzled.

'Because I don't want to inconvenience my fellow travellers, as they would have had to wait for me to return, probably thinking I'd got waylaid or lost.'

'But if they'd seen that note straight away, they might have intercepted you,' he replied somewhat disbelievingly.

'I was already gone!' I exclaimed with a smile.

London is a big place with lots of visitors, lots of British police and not somewhere where ŠtB could have grabbed me in broad daylight in any event.

***

Through my Italian production contacts, I managed to get a plane ticket delivered to Martin at his Venice hotel on July 12th – he knew to expect an envelope and knew not to breathe a word to anyone. He was to take a taxi the next morning, at the crack of dawn, to catch the 8am flight to London – hopefully before anyone else in his group woke up and noticed he was missing.

It was five days between my arrival in London and his, and meanwhile, I had no way of knowing if he was even in Venice or if he'd got the plane ticket. There were so many things that could have gone wrong, and I was relying on every single element of the plan to slot into place – and on time.

With Frank's help, I had an appointment and thus reported to the UK Home Office, where I explained I was seeking political asylum. They were efficient, polite, but of course very serious in their approach to ascertaining who I was, why I'd chosen to flee Prague, and, I guess, to ensure I wasn't some sort of spy or troublemaker.

I already knew I would need to support myself on arriving, and it was made very clear that there were no government handouts, no free accommodation to move into and certainly no healthcare or other benefits. But that was OK, I didn't expect to be greeted with open arms – I knew I'd have to make and earn my own way.

The offices were located in Croydon, a town 9 miles south of central London, and I remember it involved a tube and a bus journey to get there. Of course, I explained my teenage son was also en route to join me.

Martin didn't speak any English or Italian, so when he slipped out of his Venice hotel and into a taxi outside, he just said the word 'airport'.

He later told me he was confused why the driver seemingly started asking questions in Italian, whilst shrugging his shoulders at Martin. What he was in fact asking was, 'which airport?' – domestic or international.

Martin didn't know how to respond but had the idea of showing the driver his ticket, and with that, they zoomed off to Marco Polo, where he passed through security and to the boarding gate unquestioned. He then presented his boarding card and passport, but the dispatcher asked 'Visa?'

When Martin couldn't produce one, they pulled him out of the queue.

I knew he didn't have a visa, and there was no way I could have got him one, as it would have involved going to the British embassy, which would have set all the alarm bells ringing.

But Martin knew he had to get on that flight and what was at risk. Understandably, he started crying – quite dramatically.

It wasn't that my planning had fallen short – quite the contrary, I chose his trip to Italy on purpose. I'd had enough experience of working with Italians to know they were not particularly thorough, and I was banking on that.

Sure enough, just as the doors to the plane were about to close, the dispatchers became fed up with the crying boy in front of them, and, realising they'd have to sit with him until the airport officials arrived, they shrugged and said, 'Go, just go!' and turned their backs.

Martin didn't hesitate and ran onto the plane with moments to spare.

I arrived at Heathrow again on July 13th with a Home Office representative and a policewoman in tow to meet Martin, as he was travelling without a visa, despite having had no communication with him and still not knowing if he'd even made the plane.

I wasn't in custody, but because I'd claimed political asylum and was in the system of being processed, I was classed as an immigrant in the UK.

I was so nervous when the kindly policewoman offered me a cup of hot sweet tea at the airport, I agreed enthusiastically, but I never realised it was traditional to drink tea with milk in England – in Prague it was only ever drunk black – so that was my first proper cuppa. I don't think it helped calm my nerves, nor please my palate.

'What will you do if he isn't on board?' the policewoman asked.

'I'll go back to Prague,' I replied matter-of-factly, knowing it would certainly mean imprisonment and indefinite separation from my mother and son.

Just then, Martin appeared through Arrivals.

CHAPTER 5

Reunited

Martin was immediately whisked to an office to be interviewed by immigration officials – well, I say 'interviewed' but of course he only spoke Czech so could only give his name and point out towards where he'd spotted me saying, 'Mum'.

The officials beckoned me over and asked me to translate with Martin. I was so happy to see him, I burst into tears. I think he was rather pleased to see me, too, after his adventure!

I explained to the immigration officers what had happened and that we both wanted to apply for political asylum to stay in the UK as refugees. I emphasised that we had left our country and were unable to go back because of the fear of persecution.

In fact as soon as the Czech authorities back in Prague realised I had stayed in London they took my mother in to be questioned, but because she seemed genuinely surprised and upset at our leaving and with her being relatively elderly, the police were not terribly interested in her; however, in my absence I was sentenced to a three year prison term and my son would have been taken to juvenile prison had they ever caught up with us.

After my earlier interview with the UK Home Office in Croydon and the initial one with Martin, I was informed that the British authorities would decide our asylum claim within six months, but meanwhile, I was cautioned that I was not allowed to work. Thankfully, I had saved some money over the three years of planning, which I knew would have to see us through – but we had to live a very basic life if I was going to eke it out.

Initially, we found what I can only describe as a horrible, horrible single hotel room in Earl's Court – an area popular with backpackers and travellers on tight budgets – which Martin and I shared, and you can imagine any 15-year-old boy wouldn't be best pleased with that prospect. We had the use of a rather disgusting communal bathroom down the corridor, but no kitchen facilities. I had to pay, as grotty as it was, what I considered an expensive weekly rent, but we didn't really have much choice.

Breakfast usually consisted of a bread roll and drink, whilst for lunch I would make a sandwich with the cheapest ingredients I could find from a supermarket, and in the evenings I'd often come up with the excuse of saying 'Oh, I'm not hungry' and would just have a biscuit or some fruit that was on the turn, whilst conjuring up something a bit more substantial for Martin. We couldn't afford restaurants or even takeaways, but we became very adept at spotting end-of-day sell-offs in grocery stores. I must admit, British food tasted very different, particularly flour and bread (horrible white sliced stuff!), and of course, there were no Eastern European food stores like you find in every town nowadays. That became a particular problem later when we moved to a house with a kitchen, where I had to adapt, experiment and make the best of bland things. But even baking my own bread proved disappointing as the flour wasn't familiar and didn't quite work in my recipes. Cheap cuts of meat, such as liver, therefore became a staple, despite us not really liking it!

Biscuits, however, became a problem.

Back home, a typical biscuit was hard, fairly tasteless and far too sweet. In Britain, there were so many wonderful different types and brands which my son and I devoured at every opportunity. Martin was very active with sport, running and burning energy generally – I was not. Consequently, after a few months, I found some of my clothes were shrinking and I couldn't fasten my trousers, so I ended up wearing loose-fitting tops as they were the only ones I could get into. What the hell was causing this problem, I wondered?

'Ah. Biscuits!'

It was a huge disappointment to us both, but they had to go. It saved us a few pounds each week, too. I needed to prioritise our finances and did not want to spend money that we might need for more pressing things later on.

Martin and I travelled through pretty much all of London, visiting the (free) landmarks, galleries, parks and museums every day – culturally it was very interesting, and I loved the rich and mixed architecture of the capital, but more importantly, it saved us from sitting in that damn depressing room. We walked for miles along the Thames through the parks and were quite gobsmacked by the vastness of the city, as back in Prague we could easily stroll from end to end in an hour or two. But in comparison, London was so much bigger and spread out. The people were all very friendly too – by and large we found them to be proud of their city and keen to ensure visitors experienced the best of it – and window shopping was wonderful, in so much as it felt as though we'd been dropped into Aladdin's Cave, though of course we couldn't afford any of it.

Frank was living in a dreary bedsit, and so set about looking for somewhere we could all share. He needed to be relatively close to the film studios, near public transport links, and a few weeks later he came back with news that there was a three-bedroom house to rent in Hayes. The Indian landlord was very nice, but the place was not the best; damp and pretty run-down. I know we came from a communist run country, but we had far, far better surroundings back home. Making the best of the situation, I set about giving the place a bit of TLC by cleaning and decorating and making the place as homely and comfortable as possible. To be fair, the landlord was so impressed that he gave us a little discount on the rent.

Thankfully, we were then able to report to the local police station, rather than going all the way to Croydon immigration offices every week, to again state what we'd been doing, if we'd been working and how we were supporting ourselves.

I had no contact with my mother nor any way of letting her know we were safe in London, as it was too dangerous to reveal ourselves to the authorities; we were still termed 'fugitives on the run'. She obviously knew we'd evaded capture when the secret police questioned her, which I know will have been a huge comfort.

Although Hayes is now a very multi-cultural area, immigrants were then viewed with suspicion and were not made to feel particularly welcome; we were foreigners with heavy accents, so we kept our heads down and ourselves to ourselves. Martin was allowed to attend English classes but wasn't allowed to enrol in school for a year, by which time he was actually fluent in his new language and sailed through.

After over six months of cleaning, decorating and sightseeing, Martin and I were finally granted 'leave to remain' on condition we continued to report at the local police station on a four-week basis.

We were eventually told there would be a court hearing soon about our status, which I thought was just part of the process. I was asked if we had a solicitor.

'Do we need one?' I enquired.

'Oh yes,' I was told, 'you should have a solicitor.'

Fair enough, I thought, imagining it would probably speed everything up.

'Don't worry,' the immigration officials assured me, 'we'll appoint someone to represent you on the day if you don't have anyone yourself.'

Again, it all sounded like a formality and just routine, so I agreed to their suggestion.

An hour ahead of our court hearing in central London, we arrived to meet our duty solicitor and told him our story. Oh, and by the way, his services were going to cost us £500 up front, which back then was an absolute fortune, and an amount we could ill afford to part with from my carefully planned budget. But what must be, must be.

'Okay,' the solicitor said, having heard everything I had to say, 'let's go in.'

From that moment on, the damn solicitor didn't say a word. He didn't open his mouth once – nothing.

My English still wasn't very good, so I couldn't really keep up with what was being said at the brief hearing, so at the end I turned to our solicitor and asked, 'What now?'

'You will be deported,' he replied matter-of-factly.

'WHAT?' I shouted, followed by a number of expletives and names which I wouldn't like to put in print now.

I was crying, quite hysterically. I accused the solicitor of taking our money whilst not even opening his mouth once – 'Who exactly are you representing?' I shouted.

'The only thing I can suggest is that you try the Canadian or Australian Embassies and see if you can settle in one of those countries,' he suggested, totally disinterested in our plight.

'Thank you very much,' I said through gritted teeth, 'for £500, that's just great advice.'

I actually did try both embassies and came away with bundles of forms, but in truth I didn't know anything about either country – apart from them being a very long way away – and didn't want to leave the UK, which I'd by then made my home for many months.

I started filling out some of the paperwork, but with tears welling in my eyes came to the conclusion we wouldn't be accepted as it was clear by the questions that they were looking to fill certain skills gaps: had I been a doctor, a nurse or even an experienced bricklayer, I might have stood a chance – but a Czech film production manager with limited English? Please!

I put the forms in the bin and became very, very emotional about the prospect of being sent back to Prague and all of the implications that would follow, including prison.

Our Indian landlord, Mr Dhillon, arrived at that moment, and seeing how upset I was, asked what had happened. I told him, and added my three years of careful plotting and planning to reach London was all about to be for nothing, all because a solicitor supposedly acting for us couldn't be bothered to speak up on our behalf.

Mr Dhillon thought for a moment and said, 'Don't worry, I have someone for you.'

'With all due respect, Mr Dhillon...' I began.

'No, he works for the Citizens' Advice Bureau, but his particular expertise is in immigration law,' he added. 'He's in Hounslow, I will introduce you.'

Crestfallen, I agreed to meet him, but when I walked into his office and saw a boy sitting there – well, a man in his 20s – my heart sank. How on earth was this youngster possibly going to help us fight the courts and a deportation order, I asked myself?

But you know what? That young man was brilliant, absolutely brilliant.

He agreed to take our case, prepared all the necessary paperwork and forms for an appeal and within a few months secured our political refugee status and an indefinite permission to stay.

To top it all, he never charged us a single penny.

Looking back, it would be easy for me to say the system was wrong, but I don't bear any grudges as I think the system was indeed right – it was our so-called legal representative who was useless.

***

I enrolled for English classes and, fortunately, found a job at Southall Community Centre, where my boss Maggie proved to be a truly lovely lady. But, although I had enough pigeon-English to get by, Maggie was Scottish with a heavy Glaswegian accent. Between my so-so grasp of English and her thick accent, it proved extremely difficult for me to understand what she was asking me to do. I was terrified of losing the job and equally terrified of having to keep asking my boss to explain, but fortunately, another staff member named Marion befriended me, and whenever Maggie was out of earshot she would explain my tasks in more decipherable tones. After a few weeks, I started to pick Maggie's accent up a little better and improved my English no end, though I think even now, forty years on, I'd probably still struggle to understand Maggie's accent totally!

Whenever I went shopping with Martin, I made a point of saying, 'No Czech talking.' I was adamant that if we were to integrate into British life, then we should speak the language at every opportunity and not be regarded as the 'foreign speaking people'. Even at home, I said we should try to speak English as much as possible – even if we got words wrong, we had to keep trying.

My English teacher urged me to strike up conversations with people in everyday life, even at bus stops. I thought that sounded a little odd – why would I start talking to absolute strangers, and what on earth would I find to talk about?

'The weather,' my teacher replied. 'British people love to chat about the weather – rain, sun, wind or grey cloud, it is always a topic of conversation!'

It took me a little while to build up my courage, but I soon discovered that anyone of any background in Britain would happily talk about the weather with me, sometimes becoming quite animated too. I suppose I was a little class-conscious in starting up conversations at first, but I soon discovered I was classless – I wasn't lower-class, middle, nor upper-class, so it didn't matter!

Fast forward eighteen years from my escape to 2003, and I received naturalisation papers and became a British citizen by swearing allegiance to the Queen on the bible at a ceremony in West London. I asked if that meant I could have both a Czech and British passport, but was told that if I wanted to be British, then I should accept that I could only hold a British passport. That's quite right, actually, I agree. I have been a proud British citizen since.

***

Back in my job at Southhall Community Centre, and about a year in, I heard of an opportunity going at the BBC's Bush House in the Strand, which was home to the World Service. The job was in their foreign broadcast department and seemed an interesting and well-paid role, interpreting and translating. I went along for an interview and was offered a role – I felt I was at long last making progress in my new life.

We were all given aliases, nicknames, and I became Suzanna. The managers explained we shouldn't use our real names for 'security purposes' – in truth, a lot of the foreign staffers were political asylum seekers like me and probably still wanted by the secret police, or equivalent, and the BBC didn't want to give us away by advertising our real identities.

It was fulfilling work, which I enjoyed, but the people, the staff, they were horrible.

My department consisted mainly of Czech staff, but they were the most arrogant know-it-alls who, far from feeling like comrades from the old country united by the fact we'd all made it out, actually resented me.

I suppose I was a new face coming in, working hard (maybe harder than them?), and they made it very clear they didn't appreciate me or my ethics. Perhaps I was being judgmental about my fellow Czechs? Or a little paranoid?

My job involved a lot of evening and late-night shifts, and I'd often find myself travelling home after midnight, on my own, across West London and out to Hayes beyond Heathrow Airport.

I felt quite nervous as there were often drunks and somewhat dubious characters on the tube, and I continually found myself looking over my shoulder. After six months, the unsociable hours coupled with the hostile nature of my Czech colleagues meant I just couldn't hack it any longer.

Yes, it was a good job with decent money, but I had a teenage son to think about and was seeing precious little of him with my long days – he was in bed when I returned home each night and was to school first thing in the morning as I was preparing to head into London. We were becoming strangers in our own home, and I was becoming increasingly unhappy.

I then discovered the Czech community in London had a meeting house in Notting Hill where all were said to be welcome. Having felt so disenfranchised at work, I thought this was it, this would be the place I'd meet like-minded Czechs who may have been on similar journeys to me, and who wouldn't perhaps feel threatened by my presence like those colleagues at the BBC... and maybe I'd find a new job?

Frank and I became members, though after a few visits, I came to realise that more and more of my fellow Czechs, who had settled well and had become established, did nothing but moan! They moaned and grumbled all the time about petty things: one girl who had a good – and lucrative – job at BBC TV Centre, along with another girl who was a script supervisor on movies, together complained about how horrible they both thought London was and how terrible the people were. I eventually snapped and said, 'If it is so terrible and you are so unhappy, then go back. Go back to Czechoslovakia.'

They looked at me with horror, as if to say 'how dare I speak out against them'. After around my fifth visit, I realised I shouldn't have been looking to establish friends in a local Czech community. No, I needed to integrate and find friends in the British community.

That summer, in a move towards this, Frank brought some of his film crew colleagues home to our house one weekend afternoon, where I prepared a big picnic. But far from being jolly and welcoming, the largely English group looked at me like I'd just crawled out from under a stone – the disdain in their faces still lives with me today. They obviously felt they were far superior to this immigrant woman with broken English who was some sort of simpleton in their eyes. Had they only known about just how hard I'd worked to reach the UK and escape communism.

Were they simply misogynists? Maybe.

But even if I had served them food on solid gold platters, they'd have still likely regarded me as being beneath them. I was terribly upset but didn't show it – I just smiled and tried to be the perfect host. Though after they'd left, I said to Frank, 'Please do not bring those people here again.'

That's all I ever said. If nothing else, the experience taught me that trying hard to integrate with British or Czech people was a mistake. No, we needed to find our own way, stop trying so hard and just make our own niche. I was sure that way we'd naturally make friends and be accepted.

But first, I needed a job.

PART TWO
THE WEST

CHAPTER 6

The Typist

Frank was still working at Pinewood Studios when he came home one evening with news:

'There is a film library called Weintraub at the studio,' he said. (They owned the archive of many British production companies, such as Ealing and ABPC Elstree and are now owned by Studio Canal). 'They are advertising for a secretary. You've worked in production. You know the business. It would be ideal and nearer to home …' he continued.

John Herron, who ran the library, invited me to go in for an interview at their warehouse-like film vaults on the backlot at Pinewood. I had, of course, been very used to working in film studios and, in whatever country or language, a film studio has an air of comfortable familiarity. I immediately felt at home.

John was a very personable, kindly man who had worked at the library for most of his life through various changes of ownership and had my CV in front of him. I could see he was making notes about my background in production, but then looked over his glasses at me and asked,

'Can you type?'

To be honest, he could have asked me if I'd flown to the moon and my answer would still be affirmative, as I needed and wanted this job so much.

'Yes, of course I can type,' I replied.

'Okay, I'll dictate a letter now and see how you get on typing it…' he suggested.

I thought for a moment and went back to my interview at Barrandov before confidently replying, 'Well, actually, it's probably better if you don't dictate now, but maybe give me your notes and tell me roughly what you want to say, and then I'll type it up and come back to you.'

'You said you could type…'

'Yes,' I replied, 'but I'm very nervous right now and wouldn't want to make a mistake.'

John looked at me a little quizzically, and despite any doubts he might have harboured, my bravado and confidence must have shone through, as he offered me the job.

He agreed he'd give me any letters he wanted typing up for me to take away, and in between filing, organising his diary and so on, I could prepare them for him to sign at the end of the afternoon in time to make the collection in the mail room.

Although the money wasn't as good as at the BBC, it was a nice company and close to home.

As Martin was getting older and growing in confidence in our new country, I also decided to take a second job, in the evenings, at Heathrow airport, where I worked in the VIP lounges as a glorified waiter. I wanted to save as much money as possible, because Frank and I had been discussing buying a house that we'd be able to share, rather than continually paying rent to live in what was quite poor accommodation. That was in the days when you could get a mortgage with a 5% deposit.

Frank and I got along well. We had briefly been but were no longer 'an item', just rather good friends. He was a bit of a dreamer, whilst I was more realistic and pragmatic, and I think the combination of both our personalities and foibles was a great strength for our little unit. At least for a while.

I valued Frank's friendship, and though we both knew it was never going to be any more than that, despite our earlier brief affair, we agreed to pool our resources and, with making a few sacrifices, found we could afford a little property in the more upmarket West Drayton area of Greater London.

Our mortgage repayments were about £600 a month, which wasn't much more than the rent we'd been paying, and as Frank had by then switched from working in the film industry to an architecture company in London, he was on a pretty good salary. There was less downtime and need for him to continually chase production work. Being a freelancer has never been easy, and with my two salaries coming in, we were able to keep our heads above water – just.

But after a few months, the cracks in our friendship began to show. I think the stress of having to continually penny pinch and watch everything we spent proved a little too much, and for whatever reason, Frank became very argumentative and also a little arrogant. His attitude spilled over into his work to the point where he wouldn't roll in to the office until maybe 10 or 11am, and he received a couple of verbal warnings about his poor timekeeping. But far from taking it on the chin, he reasoned that he was happy to stay until 8pm or even 9pm and therefore couldn't see what the issue was.

His boss said it was not setting a good example to the other staff who were at their desks by 9am, and besides which, when he went home at 5.30pm, he had no way of knowing what Frank was doing or how much work he was getting through. Frank didn't heed the warnings. One evening, he arrived home and told me he'd been fired.

In a way, it didn't surprise me, but there we were with a new house and a big mortgage, and the worst of it was that Frank didn't seem that concerned.

'Why were you fired?' I asked.

'I don't know,' he shrugged.

Of course, I knew why, but it seemed pointless trying to discuss it with him as Frank's arrogance and disdain was becoming more and more evident.

I couldn't afford to pay the mortgage on my own, but I wasn't prepared to accept defeat after months and months of hard work and all our scrimping and saving. The thought of losing our home was not an option, so I told Frank I would go to see his boss the next day. I felt as if I could just explain how important his employment was to us all, and how I would make sure he bucked up his ideas and promised he would be in the office by 9am every single morning, then he might just give Frank another chance. It was worth a try at least.

I arrived at the architecture firm in Kensington, dressed very businesslike, and put across my case… I pleaded, and guaranteed that Frank would not put a foot out of line again and would be the most punctual member of staff ever, as he realised our lovely new home was at risk and how we'd settled there so well, and that Martin was happy at the local school etc. I laid it all pretty thick, to be honest.

But as nice as the boss was, he simply wasn't for being swayed.

'It's not that I'm unsympathetic,' he said, 'but I have given Frank so many chances… No, I'm sorry, I can't give him yet another chance. It's too much.'

Crestfallen, I returned to work at Weintraub, wondering what the hell we were going to do – it was nearly Christmas 1990, and we were probably going to be homeless. I had to try and put a brave face on things, whilst frantically worrying about what might come next.

Meanwhile, I realised the Czech Secret Police had found where we were – they didn't visit the house but were very obviously watching from the corner of the road. A tall figure could often be seen lurking, smoking cigarettes and keeping watch. I'd been around ŠtB agents at Barrandov enough to spot them and their methods.

I thought very carefully about who might have given us away, and the only possible two conclusions I could come up with was either when I was working at the BBC World Service, where fellow Czechs weren't particularly warm nor welcoming, so maybe one of them was informing the Secret Police or somehow giving them access to staff records where they found names and addresses, including mine. Or secondly, it might have been through Frank doing some design work for a Czech chap who we later discovered worked at the Embassy, which of course was staffed by ŠtB – obviously, he had Frank's address, and if they put two-and-two together about Frank and his Czech 'family' then that might have given us away. That seemed the more likely of the two.

Though the fact that they were only observing rather than trying to intercept or arrest us made me think they were perhaps more interested to see if we'd defected and were passing on state secrets (as though I had any!). In that case, they'd be keener on discovering who our 'contact' was.

We were all cautious when we left the house each day, making sure we weren't followed – we'd move into more crowded areas, or busy carriages on the tube. We were careful about who we were seen with and were much more guarded about conversations.

After a few weeks, the observers realised we weren't doing anything very interesting at all and must have grown fed up with watching and following us.

It was at this point that Paul Hitchcock re-entered my life.

Paul appreciated and valued my work and said that I should 'look him up' if I was ever in London or needed any introductions – as so many people often do but never mean, of course.

I thought maybe it was time to 'look him up' and put a call through to his secretary, Julie, at the Warner bungalow located in the studio's ornate gardens. I explained that I'd worked at Barrandov and had met Paul before, asking if I could make an appointment to see him for a catch-up chat.

A short time afterwards, Julie called back to say Paul wondered if I would like to go to their Christmas gathering the next day, where he'd be delighted to have a chat. I obviously sounded a little unsure and confessed to Julie, 'I won't know anyone there.'

In the run-up to Christmas, all the talk was about the annual Warner Bros. party and how it was always the best of the best. Paul was the boss and therefore the host.

'It's ok, Paul will be delighted to see you – please come,' Julie replied.

But won't you know, the next day there was also the Weintraub end-of-year party, and that wasn't going to be at the studio but rather about 8 miles away at a restaurant in Uxbridge. How could I be in two places at once? I obviously couldn't miss our gathering, particularly after John Herron had been so kind in giving me a chance in the job, but equally, I realised how rude it would seem if I turned Paul down.

The next day, I said I'd join my colleagues in Uxbridge a while later, before first heading over to the Warner bungalow with a big bunch of flowers for Julie. I didn't know anyone there but made some pleasantries, and then Paul spotted me.

'Lidia! What on earth are you doing in Pinewood?' he asked warmly.

I told him how we'd escaped and that I now had a job on the other side of the studio lot. I think he was slightly shell-shocked to not only see me there but also hear my much better English and that I was now literally working across the road from him!

I made my apologies and said I had to dash as it was the office Christmas lunch and I was expected, but that it was lovely to see him again.

'You must stay, and I'll introduce you to people…' he suggested. 'Where are you going?'

'Uxbridge,' I replied.

'Oh, well that's much posher than here, so I can understand why you'd want to get off,' he replied disappointedly.

'What, Uxbridge?' I queried.

'Oh! Sorry, with all the background chatting, I misheard you. I thought you said Knightsbridge!' (Better English but still a strong accent!)

'Leave me your number and I'll call you in January – it'll likely be towards the end of the month as I have to go to LA – but I will call, and we'll have a proper catch-up.'

CHAPTER 7

Warner Bros.

True to his word, Paul called me in the new year for a catch-up, and not being one to beat about the bush, he said I was wasting my time at Weintraub and should return to production.

'Well, yes, that is easier said than done,' I told him. 'I'd love to, but I don't know the system here, my English still isn't perfect…'

'Bullshit. Bullshit!' he replied. 'You are a brilliant assistant! Look, I'll need you in the summer on a picture. I can't offer you a job now, but on this production you'll be perfect!'

'That'd be wonderful, Paul, but I'd have to give Weintraub notice…'

'Then give them notice now,' he said.

'But what if the film doesn't happen?' I cautiously queried, having been around the business long enough to know that there's no such thing as a certainty.

'It will happen; it is happening. Give in your notice.'

I was too nervous to walk away from a steady job, so I didn't say anything to John Herron, but three months later, in April, Paul phoned to say he needed me to start on the movie for Warner's in June.

'Oh, Paul, I haven't given notice to the Weintraub library, and my contract states it has to be 6 months …'

'But I told you to hand in your notice in January,' Paul replied.

'I know, I know. But I didn't.'

'What is your boss' name?' Paul asked. I told him, and Paul said he would phone John and picked up another line and dialled… I heard him saying, 'You don't need Lidia, John, but I do, and I need her to start in June. Can you please release her from her contract?' It seemed like déjà vu for a minute, with Dermacol.

John obviously said he would need to find a replacement first, before he could consider letting me go, but Paul cut to the chase:

'John, we'll meet in the bar at lunchtime for a drink and will agree that Lidia will join Warner Bros. in June. Okay with you?'

John was a terribly nice man, and Paul could be very persuasive, so between the two of them, it was all agreed, very amicably, just like that. Sure enough, in June, I started and my first assignment was to fly to Italy to meet Oscar-winning Czech director Jiří Menzel who Warner Bros. wanted desperately to direct their next film for them, following his 1987 Academy Award nomination for *My Sweet Little Village* (and after his win two decades earlier for *Closely Watched Trains*).

Menzel didn't speak a word of English, and consequently, it had proven extremely difficult for any of the studio executives to communicate with him; and attempted conversations usually ended with the director putting the phone down on them in embarrassment.

Paul had the idea of sending me to meet Menzel on his vacation in a town north of Venice called Udine and assured me that all my travel and accommodation would be taken care of, and all I had to do was stay until Menzel said 'yes'. 'Don't come back until he does!' Paul added.

I flew to Marco Polo and looked around the terminal with a lump in my throat, thinking this huge airport was where Martin negotiated his way through to London just a few years before. The Italian representative of Warner Bros., Mario Pisani, met me. He was extremely pleasant and handed me details of my hotel, gave me a per diem in Lira (out of pocket expenses) and put me on a coach, which was the only way of reaching the fairly remote town.

Menzel obviously chose Udine for a reason – to avoid visitors!

He certainly played hard to get and wouldn't initially meet with me, but because he eventually realised we had something in common in that we were two Czechs in a foreign country – and that I wasn't going anywhere until I saw him – he gave in and came to my hotel. Paul's gamble on hiring me had seemingly paid off, though my initial optimism was short-lived.

'Lidia, I cannot make a film for an American studio,' he told me in Czech. 'I do not speak English, and it is very impractical to work through interpreters on a film set, do you understand? I am not learning another language either,' he said quite emphatically. He simply wasn't interested, and no amount of money or control would seemingly sway him.

After five days of failing to tempt and persuade Menzel, I called Paul with an update:

'Unfortunately, he will not make the movie, Paul,' I explained forlornly. 'You have to understand his reasoning: he would need to be in charge of the floor, and without speaking English he would find that impossible, and it really would not be a happy experience for a director of his calibre.'

Paul understood. I'd given it my best shot, and after all, not everyone – English speaking or otherwise – wanted to work for an American studio on big-budget films.

(Menzel made just half a dozen more films as a writer/director, mainly in Czech, and one Russian-Czech-British co-production towards the end of his life called *The Life and Extraordinary Adventures of Private Ivan Chonkin* (1994), on which I was production manager as it happens because I was able to travel to the Czech Republic again by then. Film work in the UK had all but dried up, so Warner Bros. allowed me to take this picture in my homeland, but would you believe he used an interpreter throughout! I'm not sure why he decided to make it, having rejected Warner Bros. a few years before… maybe he needed the money at that point? Nevertheless, he drove the British producer Eric Abraham crazy by continually falling behind schedule, blaming language barriers, and generally being very difficult over so many little things. In fact, it was as if he didn't want to be involved with the film at all.)

But, I was, of course, deeply concerned about returning to London without the 'yes' Paul wanted as it might have meant the end of my job. But I needn't have worried as, without missing a beat, when I reported back to the office Paul said, 'I know you're more qualified, but that was in a different country and in a different language, but if you'd be willing to work as an assistant, helping out as needed, then a full-time job is still yours.'

I accepted without hesitation.

***

My son Martin was at this point doing his exams at school, where, fortunately, he achieved really high marks and was destined for great things. You can therefore imagine my horror when he said, 'Mum, I would like to go to film school.'

'No, you're not,' I told him, 'You are either going to be a doctor or lawyer, you are not following in my or your father's footsteps.'

But when he turned 18, he remained adamant that's what he wanted, so I couldn't stop him. In fact, my reluctance to let him pursue a career in movies made him all the more determined to get a scholarship to Poole University (1989-1992), and he became more and more enthusiastic. Through Paul, he was offered some intern work at Warner Bros. at the time when they were moving archives, and Martin was asked to help sort out the files. He was so efficient that, after only a week, he had everything catalogued, sorted into boxes and ready to transport. Paul had agreed he could have a few weeks' placement, so he stood scratching his head about how he was going to keep Martin busy for the rest of the time.

He then arranged for Martin to work as a runner on a film shooting at Pinewood, and on his last day the production manager spoke to Martin about what he might like to do in the film business, 'You see that person over there, organising everyone and "shouting" around the set – that's the job I want!' was his reply.

He was referring to the First Assistant Director.

Martin has done extremely well since, including obtaining a BA Hons degree in Media Production and has risen through the ranks, working on many big Hollywood productions as an assistant director. He has recently worked with Steven Soderbergh.

***

The Berlin Wall had fallen, and the 'Velvet Revolution' had taken place in my home country in November '89 and brought about a non-violent transition of power, resulting in the end of decades of one-party rule – the Czech Republic having been born.

You will recall that just before I escaped Czechoslovakia, I paid a Major to look after three suitcases for me, and though Paul was familiar with my story of escaping with just one small suitcase, I somehow managed to live without anything more from the home country, and the subject of other belongings never came up. Then one particular day, probably sparked by something we were talking about, I mentioned to Paul that all my documents and lovely clothes were still in a German village. I guess I hadn't quite figured out how I was going to get them from East Germany, as I only had an address, and to be honest, I never even knew if the guardians even existed.

After the revolution, things seemed to start changing for the better and for the first time since my escape, I thought it might be possible to try and retrieve my three suitcases. I knew it would need someone to physically travel to this village on the border with former East Germany and pick them up – but I wasn't about to risk flying into a recently communist controlled area where I might have still been on a wanted list. With corruption probably still being what it was, it was a very real possibility that I might be turned in. Who to? I didn't really know, but there were still dark powers lurking in the shadows as some in Russia weren't particularly overenthusiastic to see its foothold slip in not only my country but also the rest of the Eastern block. Outwardly, Russia said it respected the people's will for change, but I'm not sure it was said wholeheartedly.

Paul suggested that if I could find someone to make the journey, then he could arrange for them to be paid, through Warner Bros. – I guess it was billed to one of their productions as recce expenses?!

At Uxbridge College, where I had enrolled to learn English, I became friends with a fellow student named Flavio, who was an Italian keen on opening a restaurant in London. I guess he reminded me of my father a little with his plans for a similar venture, so when he told me money was very tight and he wasn't sure he could pay his rent, I suggested Frank and I could offer him our spare bedroom for a while – for a nominal fee, of £10 or thereabouts – and in fact he ended up staying seven months.

Anyhow, I thought maybe my Italian friend could do with a bit of extra cash, so I asked if he fancied a trip to Germany.

He didn't need asking twice, and even said he'd figure out the route and method of travel, and all I'd have to do was arrange for his expenses and an agreed fee, and he'd keep me posted.

Flavio duly set off, and for four days I never heard a word from him. Of course, it crossed my mind he might have just taken the money, or worse still, taken my suitcases, and done a runner. As much as I liked our lodger, I couldn't help but fear the worst after such a seemingly long radio silence. However, I needn't have worried as he returned carrying my beloved luggage, and I felt so relieved, so joyful and so grateful to him.

I burst into tears, barely registering his explanation of how he had to fly in to a small airport somewhere in the old East Germany, then endure a long train journey followed by two buses to reach the town in question – the name of which I forget, after thirty-odd years – where making a trunk call to London proved impossible. There, in a garage, covered in dusty old blankets, lay my belongings, all intact and all just as I had packed them. The mysterious Major had been true to his word. I had paid him quite a lot of money (around the equivalent of £1000), never really knowing if he was trustworthy.

Some of Martin's schoolbooks, clothes and shoes were amongst the luggage, though they weren't of much use to him by then!

I didn't return to the Czech Republic until 1992, but my mother was meanwhile able to travel to the UK after the Berlin Wall fell in November 1989. She loved it here with all the sights, sounds and culture. So much so, I tried to persuade her to move to be near me and her grandson, but she would not have any of it.

'Lidia, I am too old to uproot and besides which I am NOT giving up my Czech state pension and allowing the government to keep it after I worked my whole life for it!'

I remember Mum saying she wanted to buy some shoes when she visited, as in Prague all you could buy were dark grey, brown or black – never any colours. So, I took her to Oxford Street, where there was shop after shop full of clothes and shoes. By the time we'd reached the third store, she still hadn't chosen a pair, and I couldn't understand why as there was literally every style and colour on display.

'What's wrong, Mum?' I asked.

She gestured for us to sit on one of the benches that lined the street, lit a cigarette and started to cry.

'Lidia, I cannot buy anything here…'

'Oh Mum, if it's the price, please do not worry as they would be my gift to you,' I replied.

'No, that's not it. I am just so overwhelmed.'

It didn't stop at shoes either, as I remember every time we passed a food or butcher's shop, she would stop to take a photograph. When I asked why, she said it was to show her friends at home, as she'd never seen such wonderful displays of food before.

I wasn't talking about visiting Harrods, or Harvey Nichols, but places like Woolworths, Etam and C&A which – if they were open today – I'd never consider as being posh or high-end. However, Mum never bought the shoes despite enjoying looking and trying them on; having lived without luxuries and treats for so many decades, it was difficult for us to adjust to such decadence, and for her in particular.

I was working a lot, and my mum wouldn't have had me around all day, nor the network of friends she enjoyed in the Czech Republic, but that didn't stop her making frequent trips to see us and staying for a few weeks at a time, during which she learnt pretty good English, as she loved doing and experiencing new things, including languages. She spoke three fluently as it was.

My mum fell ill in 1992, and I flew out to be with her. Despite her failing health, she could see I was not really happy and told me I should leave Frank and move on with my life. It was almost as though I was repeating what had happened with my husband, as we had been living separate lives for a long time but stayed together for the sake of – in this case – the mortgage. It certainly wasn't a recipe for happiness.

Mum sadly passed away in 1993, and it led to Frank and me splitting up as the frequency of our disagreements increased; my mother's death was a big wake-up call to me. Frank was all about looking after number one, and many was the time he would say how he'd really like to marry a British woman for 'passport and money' – love never came into it – that really gave me the push I needed.

'Listen, I want to buy you out,' I said to him in a pique of frustration. Quite how I would have been able to afford it, I don't know! He initially refused, but not too long afterwards, he met a Czech woman and the relationship started getting quite serious quite quickly. She was keen that Frank make the split so they could live together, and he moved out, which suited him nicely as it happens.

***

Incidentally, when my mum came to England on one of those later-life visits, she said, 'Oh, I have brought something for you, from Prague!'

'What's that?' I asked excitedly.

'Your wedding invitation. I found them. You never told me!' she laughed.

I explained the whole charade…

CHAPTER 8

Stanley Kubrick

From 1991, I did pretty much anything and everything at Warner Bros., from making the tea to assisting in day-to-day business meetings. One of the big projects at that time was a film adaptation of Andrew Lloyd-Webber's *Phantom of The Opera*, which was being lined up to shoot in the Czech Republic – so that was right up my street.

The studio had purchased the film rights in early 1989, and Lloyd-Webber (who had total creative control) hired Joel Schumacher to direct and co-wrote the screenplay with him. Michael Crawford and Sarah Brightman had agreed to reprise their roles from the original stage production, and filming was originally set to begin at Pinewood in July 1990. However, it was then pushed back a couple of months to November because of Lloyd-Webber and Sarah Brightman's divorce, and then transferred to Barrandov Studios in Prague where there were considerable cost efficiencies but, in the event, protracted divorce settlements, coupled with the director's career taking off following the release of *Flatliners* (1990), pushed the project into development limbo and the film didn't get made until 2004.

Warner Bros. had a busy release schedule with their own productions, co-productions and pick-ups – films they didn't finance but purchased the distribution rights for, such as *The Witches*, *Reversal of Fortune*, and *Men Don't Leave* – with marketing and release strategy being handled mainly from LA.

There were, however, many projects that the studio had either optioned or were developing which never progressed into production despite months (sometimes years) and considerable funds being invested. One being *Fade-Out* for David Puttnam's Enigma Productions.

Puttnam had re-established a development deal with Warner Bros., following his ill-fated tenure as Head of Columbia Pictures in LA. I assisted Paul Hitchcock in dealing with writers, recceing locations and coming up with schedules, budgets and casting ideas.

Puttnam's director colleague Hugh Hudson (with whom he collaborated on *Chariots of Fire*) was meanwhile developing a separate film with the studio called *Homage to Catalonia*: a true story about George Orwell and his wife Eileen, and the effect their encounter with Georges Kopp – the commander of the Anarchist brigade that Orwell joined during the Spanish Civil War – had on both of them. For various reasons, neither film made it into production, though Hudson continued to nurture the project and, at the Cannes Film Festival in 2009, almost two decades later, announced Colin Firth and Kevin Spacey were attached to play Orwell and Kopp, with shooting scheduled during the first half of 2010 in England and Spain. Again, it didn't happen. But that's nothing new in the film business, where projects and scripts can languish for years, despite having a fortune spent on them.

The same was the case with *The Count of Monte Cristo*, which Warner Bros. began setting up in 1993. It was to be an all-star adaptation of Alexander Dumas' classic novel, but for one reason or another, it didn't go ahead, and in fact took another studio, Touchstone Pictures (Disney), to pick it up from 'turnaround' after paying off Warner Bros.' expenditure. I could probably write a book about all the projects that got away or never made it off the starting blocks; however, they were the lifeblood of the studio creative process and certainly kept us all busy.

Perhaps most significantly in 1993, though, Warner Bros.' favourite director, Stanley Kubrick, announced that *Aryan Papers* was to be his next movie. Having long harboured an ambition to make a movie about World War II and the Holocaust, he optioned Louis Begley's novel 'Wartime Lies' which centred on the experience of a boy and his aunt living in hiding under false identities in Nazi-occupied Poland.

Kubrick wrote the first draft screenplay himself, with rumours he was considering Julia Roberts or Uma Thurman as the aunt, and he meanwhile decided the Czech Republic and Slovakia would make the ideal filming locations.

'It will never happen,' Paul said matter-of-factly to me, 'as Stanley will never travel.'

Nevertheless, I was assigned to the project to translate, check that all of the location descriptions were accurate and to travel to them where I and other production personnel engaged in various meetings, including with lawyers in Bratislava.

Phil Hobbs (Stanley's son-in-law) and Jan Harlan (his brother-in-law) came along as his producers – but without Stanley himself! – and I mainly travelled around with Roy Walker, our production designer, and Chris Brock, the location manager.

As Paul had warned, Stanley refused to travel. He hated leaving his home, let alone the UK, and had a total aversion to flying – as was the case when he first arrived in London in the early 1960s by boat – but Jan Harlan insisted Stanley was willing to relocate, albeit with great hesitation.

My first meeting with Stanley on *Aryan Papers* was almost disastrous, for me at least. It was held at Jan Harlan's home, and Stanley said he wanted the top Czech production manager on board, who was a really lovely guy, but he didn't speak any English. I arrived at the house to interpret and instinctively greeted Stanley with a kiss on the cheek and said how pleased I was to be there.

I then sat next to Phil Hobbs, who hissed at me – a really nasty hiss.

'You *never* do that again!'

'Do what? What do you mean?' I asked.

'You were *so* personal with Stanley. You kissed him!!'

'But that's how I've always greeted colleagues and friends,' I reasoned, thinking it perfectly normal.

'No! Don't you ever do that again, or you're out.'

Phil Hobbs was very protective of Stanley. By trade, he was a film caterer and then married Katharina Kubrick – Stanley's daughter and film art director – and I guess he felt his subsequent promotion to a 'producer' role meant he should behave like an important producer... only most of the best producers are nice, kind and above all humble people. He clearly never got that memo.

The meeting went on for quite a few hours and Stanley liked Roman, the Czech production manager, but it became obvious that he would really need an English speaking PM otherwise it would be hugely impractical and time consuming for both of them to communicate via interpreters – it was at that moment that I totally understood what Jiří Menzel had meant when he declined to take on that Warner Bros. film I had pursued him for.

As I was leaving the meeting, Stanley remained sitting at the head of the table. I said goodbye to everyone and smiled slightly towards him without wishing to overstep the mark that Phil had firmly pushed me behind.

'What? No kiss this time?' Stanley asked mischievously.

I went over and gave him a peck on the cheek as Phil looked on, but of course, he dared not say anything to me as it was at Stanley's instigation. If anyone was put in their place that day, it was Phil Hobbs!

I developed a nice rapport with Stanley afterwards: initially, it was very businesslike and quite serious. For instance, Stanley asked I translate sections of his script and then make various copies on his new Xerox machine. He always made a point of getting the newest, most advanced technology, and this extended to the photocopier, which I stared at with equal amazement and confusion: it was the biggest, most complicated piece of equipment ever, and I had no idea where to even start, let alone make numerous copies.

Just at that moment, I spotted Emilio D'Alessandro, Stanley's driver. Well, to be fair, Emilio was much more than a driver; he was Stanley's right-hand man.

'I don't know what to do,' I stammered to him.

Seeing the panic in my eyes, Emilio smiled and came over to show me... just as Stanley appeared and asked what he was doing.

'I'm showing Lidia how to operate the machine...'

'If she doesn't know how to use it, then she shouldn't be here,' he snapped.

Stanley certainly didn't suffer fools, and I was worried about putting a toe, let alone a foot, wrong from that point on.

But as the weeks went by, we spent more and more time together at his home, which was also his office (thus allowing him to write off expenses against tax). One day, he asked me, 'What do you do for lunch?'

'I have a sandwich at my desk in the office,' I replied.

'Why don't you join me in the kitchen?' he suggested. 'And we can talk about your country.'

'Don't you want to have lunch with your wife?' I enquired.

'No, Christiane is always painting. Come, come and chat with me...' and he prepared sandwiches whilst talking and asking me questions about my homeland. They were very specific too, such as 'what type of trees dominate Prague' and 'how do the trees in the Czech Republic differ from ones in Slovakia', plus about plants, grass and terrain. Stanley was an extremely interesting man, very well read and took a great interest in so very many things, and consequently a great fount of knowledge. I enjoyed our friendly lunchtime discussions hugely as he was genuine in all he asked, and he eagerly listened and sought opinions.

One lunchtime, he was obviously in a rather jovial mood. 'Lidia, you see this bread and you see this milk?' he asked as he produced our snack.

'Yes?' I replied, wondering where this particular discussion was going.

'Well,' he chuckled, 'isn't it wonderful that Warner Bros. pay for it all?!'

Warner's did indeed sign the cheques for pretty much everything that they received the bills for, as that was the relationship Stanley had with the studio, who in return waited patiently for the next Kubrick masterpiece.

During my second or third week of commuting to Childwickbury Manor, Stanley's manor house located just outside St Albans, I realised I was using quite a lot of petrol. Admittedly, I had a really fun sports car, a convertible MG (which I was paying for on Hire Purchase), but the 40-mile-a-day commute each way, six-days-a-week, was costing considerably more than my usual trip to Pinewood, so I plucked up the courage to have a word with Phil Hobbs.

'I wonder if it might be possible, if I could have a fuel allowance as I'm really travelling a long way every day...'

'Is it in your contract?' he asked earnestly.

'No.'

'What are you being paid?' he enquired.

'£500 a week,' I replied – knowing full well it was a very generous wage for those days.

'Then the answer is no!' he said.

'OK, no problem, Phil, I just thought I'd ask. But no problem, forget I even mentioned it,' I replied.

Afterwards, I thought to myself, hang on, it's not Phil's money or even Kubrick's money – it's Warner Bros.' and they probably wouldn't have even flinched. I dare say Phil Hobbs thought he was doing the production a favour, saving them £20 or £30 a week!

Paul Hitchcock had worked with Stanley on several pictures, but I was curious as to why he always used to say, 'Warner Bros. love announcing a new Kubrick film... but they hate making it!'

I soon saw, first hand, what he meant...

Approaching Easter, and on the Thursday prior to the holiday weekend, Stanley called us all together in his office and said:

'We are so close to production,' (oh yeah?!), 'and we have a four-day week this week and next, and we can't afford to lose so much time. So, I'd like to ask if you'd consider working on Easter Monday?'

He looked at Phil Hobbs, who lived 5 minutes away from Stanley's house, 'Of course I will!' he exclaimed with a sycophantic smile.

Then he glanced at Roy Walker, our production designer, who said, 'OK, I don't have a problem with that.'

But Eric Rattray, the Associate Producer, said: 'Oh Stanley, I can't. We have all the family coming for a big lunch on Monday, and it'd be too difficult for me to cancel at short notice.'

'No, that's fine, that's fine,' Stanley assured him.

He then looked at me, 'How about you, Lidia, you have family?'

'I can come, Stanley; I don't have any particular plans.'

'Ah, good. Thank you, everyone, have a nice weekend,' he concluded with a warm smile.

Roll on Easter Monday, and we all carried on with our work, though we were told to come in a little later, which was appreciated. We even wrapped a bit earlier, too.

On Tuesday, we all arrived in the office, that is apart from Eric, who was seemingly running late... 10.30am... 11am... but there was still no sign of him.

I asked Roy if he'd seen Eric.

'He's not coming,' he replied.

'Why not?' I asked.

'You haven't heard? Stanley phoned him last night and asked him how Easter went... Eric said it was very enjoyable and he was very appreciative of Stanley for letting him spend the day with his family.'

'Awww. That's nice,' I added.

'And then Stanley told him he could spend a lot more time with his family, as he was fired.'

Stanley had total – and I mean TOTAL – control over every aspect of a project to the point where he wouldn't even discuss it with studio executives, let alone let them see a script or a budget (though I don't think there ever was such a complete thing). It was more a case of Warner's just sending cheques over until a film was finished and presented to them. Quite often, senior executives at the studio would have no idea what the film was about, nor would they be allowed to see any footage; it must have been very frustrating for them, but they just had to be patient and wait. That's why I think Paul said they found the announcement more exciting than the production process.

One day, Stanley came into a production meeting and said, 'Spielberg is working on a similar project and I'm not going to compete with him!'.

That marked the end of our film, just like that.

Stanley felt *Schindler's List* had similar themes to his script, though he cautioned, 'The medium of cinema is totally inadequate for capturing the sheer horror and scope of the Holocaust.'

Whatever his real reasons, it left him free to return to the *A.I. Artificial Intelligence* film project he was nurturing closer to home – he never made that either, but some years later, Steven Spielberg did.

Aryan Papers was one of several projects Stanley developed – often for years – but for one reason or another failed to move into production. A few of his others that fall into that category were an aborted *Napoleon* biopic, *The German Lieutenant*, in which a group of German soldiers embark upon a mission during the final days of World War II, *Artificial Intelligence* (which I've mentioned Spielberg later made) and even a new version of *Pinocchio*. His ideas and ambitions were wide and varied, and often only abandoned at a very advanced stage.

***

My mum died in January 1993. I think she was looking out for me from 'up there' as my relationship with Frank finally ended, which turned out to be a real blessing – well aside from all the loans and debts he left behind – and my career had taken a good turn when I was appointed as Producers' Assistant to Paul Hitchcock, added to which my son Martin had graduated from university and came home to join me (and my two cats). On a personal level, things really were very good.

On a professional level, however, there was very little happening in the UK film industry, which was in one of its regular slumps. My workload had lightened so much that when British producer Eric Abraham approached me, saying he was making a film in the Czech Republic with Jiří Menzel and needed a bilingual production manager and queried if I would be interested in joining him, I thought about it very carefully. It was *The Life and Extraordinary Adventures of Private Ivan Chonkin* (1994).

I asked Paul if I could be released for a few months to work on the project and, after expressing some initial reluctance, he agreed. Maybe he thought I wouldn't come back? Maybe he thought there wouldn't be much work for us at Warner Bros. if the slump continued? Paul also knew I was trying to sort out the financial problems Frank had left behind, whilst also taking over the mortgage on the house. In fact, I took legal advice about the various threatening letters from debt collectors and the threat of bailiffs descending, and thankfully, I was reassured as these were personal (unsecured) debts and, as Frank and I never married, then they were not my concern, and I was told to ignore all bully-boy harassment tactics. It wasn't easy, but I was tenacious!

Anyway, it was wonderful to be back in my homeland working on a movie in a position I'd trained for and had gone through so very much since making my last film there.

On set one day during the shoot, a runner came to find me and said, 'Lidia, there is someone on the phone for you.'

'Who?' I asked rather impatiently, as I was up to my eyes in things.

'I don't know. Someone called Kubrick, I think he said…'

Ahhh. The innocence of youth. The young guy had no idea who he had been speaking with!

'Of course!' I laughed. 'It could only be Stanley…' and I returned to the production office to take his call. Quite how he'd tracked me down, I don't know, but without much in the way of pleasantries, he launched straight into the purpose of his call.

'Lidia, I need to speak to Nik Korda. I think he's in Germany.'

'But Stanley, I'm on set…' I reasoned.

'Lidia, I'll call you back in three hours,' he continued, totally uninterested in my protestation, 'if you could get me his number, please.'

'Okay, Stanley,' I replied, realising he wouldn't ever accept 'no' for an answer, so I excused myself and asked my assistant to take over whilst I made some calls. I managed to track Nik Korda, who was a production manager and assistant director, and called him.

'Stanley Kubrick is looking for you. May I give him this number?' I asked a rather bemused Korda.

He agreed, and, sure enough, Stanley phoned back three hours later.

'Have you found him?' he asked impatiently.

'Of course, I have Stanley…' and I gave him the number.

I think that was the last time I heard from Stanley. Tom Cruise did invite the UK crew (of which I was one) to watch a preview screening of *Eyes Wide Shut* – Stanley's last film – during the shoot of *Mission: Impossible 2*. Tom was eager to hear Paul's thoughts, though.

Paul was very diplomatic in his response as he did not want to hurt his star's feelings by saying it was dreadful, but he later confided in me that he felt it was a mistake for Stanley to have made such an erotic story. You see, Stanley's self-imposed reclusiveness meant that he really did not have any understanding of the real world apart from what he read or saw on TV and films, and a subject such as this wasn't a natural and comfortable fit for him.

Nevertheless, I was quite chuffed that he had called me, though I don't think the runner ever lived it down – the day he spoke to Stanley Kubrick and didn't even realise.

CHAPTER 9

First Knight

With Pinewood's stages quiet, I was conscious that I had a large mortgage and if there were to be layoffs within Warner Bros., I realised I could be dispensable. But then again, having done so many courageous things in my life by that point, and with Paul having been with Warner's since 1969 as a senior executive, I actually felt fairly comfortable and excited about the future. However, what I hadn't banked on was the curveball Paul threw – he was approaching his 60th birthday, and although he still had two years to run on his contract, he came in one day and said, 'I really don't want to do this anymore.'

He wasn't enjoying the job any longer and thought it was time to call it a day. The UK film industry, which the Conservative government of the time had little to no interest in supporting, meant production activity in Britain had slowed down to a level that Paul had become less and less directly involved in what he loved doing – making films. He rang his boss, Terry Semmel, in LA and asked if they could meet; the following week, Paul arrived at his Burbank office.

'I know it is no good for me nor the company to keep going,' Paul confessed.

Terry was surprised and, of course, suspected Paul might have received an offer from another company. But no, Paul reaffirmed he simply wanted to retire, and his 60th birthday seemed the most appropriate time. You can imagine I was not at all pleased to hear the news – and that is putting it mildly!

Paul agreed to stay on as a consultant, to see out his contract, though it wasn't a particularly fulfilling time as Paul realised the worst job to have is as a 'consultant' because the people coming into the position he'd left didn't want to hear how he would have handled things and he became so frustrated in not having any control or authority that it proved a bit of a pointless and thankless role.

We moved out of the Warner Bros. bungalow and into a new office in Pinewood's main administration building, with me all the time wondering what would happen after the two-year consultancy period ended.

Just before that looming date arrived, Gary Martin, the head of Production for Sony-Columbia, phoned and explained he had a problem on a movie that was about to start shooting at Pinewood called *First Knight*. He asked if Paul was free and interested in taking it over.

That single call transformed Paul from a disenfranchised consultant to an independent producer – and I was about to become very busy again as his right-hand woman.

First Knight was a big-budget feature centred around the King Arthur and Camelot legend, starring Sean Connery, Richard Gere and Julia Ormond. To begin with, Gary Martin, Eric Rattray (the Line Producer whom I knew from *Aryan Papers*), and director Jerry Zucker met with Paul to give him a feel for the problems they felt they were up against in the fervent hope he could swiftly bring things back on track.

Paul was furious to hear they'd fired the production designer John Box because someone in accounts said his sets were over budget – and that was one of their big problems, they reckoned.

'If anyone needs John Box on this picture you do,' Paul explained, 'but the thing with John is that you need him to have an art director and construction manager who know how to manage their costs, as John will design you the best garden shed in the world but if you asked him how much it cost to build he'd have no idea.'

Much to the delight of the crew, John Box was reinstated.

Paul studied the budget and schedule they'd been working with, and it soon became clear that both had been underestimated.

Jerry Zucker had only ever really directed comedy films at this point in his career, and *First Knight* was a very serious drama, with lots of setups, masses of action and complicated dialogue. Jerry was panicking he was going to fall behind from day one, as he'd never had such a tight timetable to work with before. Plus, added into the equation were two huge, demanding stars (and egos) to deal with. Sean Connery didn't suffer fools, and if he felt the director didn't have total control and confidence, then he could be tricky.

After Paul instigated a few adjustments to the schedule, the team seemed much happier and more confident that they could deliver the film.

Next, I thought it would be a nice gesture from Paul, coming on board as the Executive Producer, to welcome our leading stars to the studio with flowers in their dressing rooms. I called a florist shop in Hayes where I knew the amazingly talented owner and explained that I wanted two of her finest 'masculine' arrangements for Sean Connery and Richard Gere, and for Julia Ormond, I wanted the most wonderfully bright, feminine arrangement of blooms possible. The florist immediately knew what I meant and started explaining what she had in mind – it was perfect!

'There is one condition, though,' she added.

'Which is?' I enquired.

'I would like to deliver them personally to Pinewood and present them, particularly to Mr Gere.'

She very obviously had a crush on him, as did most ladies, it must be said.

Sure enough, she dutifully reported to the studio the next morning at 8am with the most wonderful flowers and waited patiently for the actors to emerge from the make-up department. But as the clock ticked towards 9am, she reluctantly explained that she had to get back to open up her shop and consequently never got to present the blooms to her heartthrob.

Incidentally, Richard was the only one who noticed and appreciated the flowers.

The main producer who had agreed the original budget and schedule was an American named Hunt Lowry. A few weeks into the film, I received a call from Sean Connery asking if Paul would go over to meet him in his dressing room. Fortunately, Paul knew Sean from their early days together at Pinewood, where he worked in the accounts department and where Sean made films such as *Hell Drivers* and the early Bond films.

'Come in, Paul, and shut the fucking door,' Sean said. 'I'm only going to tell you this once – I am NOT going on the set if Hunt Lowry is there. If he wants to go on set when I'm not, and it's just Gere, fine, but if he walks on and I'm there, then that's it – I'm going home.'

Hunt Lowry was a perfectly pleasant man, though had seemingly upset Sean by arriving on set at 10.30am – long after all the actors and crew had arrived and all the decisions had been made – and proceeding to make a series of phone calls, usually to his wife about dinner arrangements, whilst sat next to Sean who was trying to get to grips with his dialogue.

Paul asked me to call Hunt and invite him over to the office.

'Why doesn't Paul come over to the set?' Hunt asked.

'No, Paul says this is very important, you HAVE to come to the office,' I told him firmly.

When Hunt arrived, Paul was blunt: 'Sean asked me to go and see him and told me under no circumstances will he go on the set if you're there.'

'What are you talking about?' Hunt laughed.

'He's told me categorically he won't work if you're there!'

Hunt walked over to Paul, put his arm around his shoulder and said, 'But Paul, I absolutely love Sean.'

'I know you do,' Paul said, wondering how he could make his point more succinctly, 'but he fucking hates you.'

There was silence for a moment before Hunt asked, 'What's the problem?'

'He says you don't concentrate on what's happening on set, you're more interested in your private life.'

'Well, I shall go and talk to Sean...' he replied.

'Hunt, I really do not think that is a good idea. Personally, if I were you, I'd leave it and keep away for a while, and I'm sure over time it will smooth out.'

He reluctantly agreed, nodded, and left the office.

Sean could be a tricky person, as I've already mentioned, and aside from disliking the producer, he obviously felt a great rivalry with Richard Gere. After all, Gere was a younger, very popular actor playing the romantic lead (the type of coveted role Sean had played for so many decades), and despite receiving top billing, Sean somehow felt relegated. He was still paid very handsomely, of course, and as he had been living outside of Britain for many years as a tax exile he got to keep most of his salary from the UK tax man, but as such he was only allowed to spend a certain number of days in the country (otherwise ALL his income would fall subject to UK tax). Therefore, Paul scheduled his scenes so that Sean could fly out late Friday afternoon to his home in Spain and then back on Monday mornings.

On returning one such Monday, Paul could see that Sean wasn't terribly happy.

'Anything I can help with?' Paul asked, fearing Hunt Lowry might have inadvertently upset the star again. Sean explained that his son Jason was making a *Harry Palmer* film in Russia for producer Harry Alan Towers, and, in the days before mobile phones were commonplace, it had proven difficult for him to get hold of his son.

'I call the hotel in St Petersburg frequently, but they don't speak English, and I'm worried that with the mafia types over there, something might have happened to him,' he lamented.

Paul said that I spoke Russian and asked if it might prove helpful if I phoned.

'Tell her to come to my office, would you?' he asked.

I walked down the long corridor past the various production offices to Sean's at the far end, knocked and entered only to find a desk lamp shining straight at me in the doorway. I thought I was about to be interrogated by the secret police.

There weren't any pleasantries; Sean just gave me the hotel number and asked if I could find out where his son was. Interrogation over.

When I got through, the receptionist explained the crew were all out on location and wouldn't be back until the following morning, which seemed to put Sean's mind at rest. Mind you, he never thanked me – I suppose I was just staff to him.

A week or two later, a relieved Sean told Paul that Jason was on his way back to London as his shoot had wrapped.

'That'll be nice for you to have him stay,' Paul suggested.

'Staying with me?!' Sean exclaimed. 'We don't have enough room.'

'But you've got the apartment in Eaton Square, haven't you?' Paul enquired.

'Yes, it only has one bedroom – purposely so people can't stay!' the canny Scot replied.

That perfectly summed up his attitude towards money. A further example of his 'thriftiness' arose when Sean quizzed Paul about his unit driver. As standard, all stars received a chauffeur-driven limo to and from the studio – usually a nice, long-wheel-based Mercedes or BMW.

'How much do you pay my driver?' Sean quizzed Paul.

'I'm not sure, why?'

'Could you find out?' Sean asked.

Paul checked and reported back. Say, for example, it was £500 a week.

'So, if I drove myself, could I have that £500?' the millionaire star enquired.

Paul was a little taken aback but couldn't think of any reason to say no, and from that day on, Sean, who was very tall at 6ft 2, arrived at the studio squeezed into an old VW Polo he was given as a free rental, seeming quite delighted he was pocketing an extra few hundred quid a week on top of his $9 million salary. Paul was just happy his star was content!

Paul's diplomacy skills came to the fore once more when we received a phone call from the studio restaurant asking him to inform Mrs Zucker that it was not 'the done thing' to change a baby's nappies on the table during lunch service. Jerry Zucker and his wife Janet had two young children, one of whom was still just a babe in arms, but how do you tell the director's wife something like that without upsetting her? Paul was very gracious about it, and I think he said something about just how prudish Brits were.

Though a man of many skills, Paul didn't have any sway with the weather – it was just *too* good.

Camelot Castle, which had been constructed on the backlot, had nothing but pure blue, cloudless skies surrounding it throughout the usually grey month of October, causing it to seem as though a large blue screen had been erected around it, which made everything look a little false.

Though I should add everything else was real, including the bread, spit roasted animals and fires on the village set which John Box designed on the Pinewood orchard; he also transformed the outdoor paddock tank to look like a giant moat – with a section of Camelot Castle on it – in order that Richard Gere, or rather his stunt double, could dive into the water from one of its towers.

Incidentally, sword-fighting sequences were CGI-enhanced, as while the actors held hilts of swords in their hands, all the blades were added in later – for safety reasons, of course.

It actually turned out to be a good movie, which came in on (revised) schedule and budget. Paul's debut as an 'independent producer' was an impressive one, though, as he was used to working at Warner Bros., where he was never allowed to take a credit, he didn't think about asking for one, so consequently was not listed as 'Executive Producer'. I felt life as an independent producer's assistant wouldn't be too bad after all.

Barrandov Studios, my place of employment for many years

The book which Barbra became obsessed with turning into a movie

Barbra behind the camera for Yentl

My mother and father on their wedding day

Me, aged 6

My graduation photograph

Alexander Dubček

Prague Spring - the invading Russian tanks

Prague Spring - Wenceslas Square

Young, carefree and happy, 1967 in Prague

With my young son Martin

*Olga Knoblochová
(known as Lady Dermacol)*

With my fellow FAMU students in 1984

Producer Jan Kadlec (my first boss) who I greatly respected, at his 50th birthday party

Barbra dedicated this signed photo to me

Production designer Peter Lamont, who went on to be extremely helpful in my escape plan

My beloved father, always dressed immaculately, even on our walks for coffee

With my former partner Frank in 1988 who, despite our later differences, made our escape possible

The rather austere ŠtB Headquarters in Prague

Westminster Abbey – the bus driver allowing us to photograph the magnificent building meant I could 'vanish' into the London crowds

Reunited with my teenage son Martin

The imposing Home Office building in Croydon

Happier times - on holiday in Spain in 1988 with Frank's aunt, Mussi

Getting to grips with sprucing up our first house in Hayes, 1985

In the garden of our house in Hayes for our first BBQ (with Martin) - a veritable Garden of Eden (not)

With my Scottish boss and first UK friend, Maggie, at a BBQ. Sadly she's no longer with us

The glamour of doing the laundry in Hayes

Christmas 1987 was a very basic affair

Roll on a decade or so – Martin and I celebrate a slightly more affluent Christmas. How things changed!

Pinewood Studios gatehouse, which I passed through every day when working at Weintraub

Paul Hitchcock – in his Pinewood office

My son Martin's graduation - imagine my horror when he said he wanted to go to film school!

On holiday with my mother in Bournemouth - getting to spend time with her again was so wonderful

On location in the Czech Republic in 1993, on 'Chonkin'

On set in 1993, on 'Chonkin'

During the shoot of 'Chonkin' with Mila, our interpreter and her son, and Paul Hitchcock visiting

Stanley Kubrick during the shoot of his final film – with Tom Cruise and Nicole Kidman, and (left) Jan Harlan

Emilio D'Alessandro, seen here with Stanley, was driver and right hand man to the film-maker and took pity on this technophobe and the photocopier!

*Paul's retirement party from Warner Bros
with Rick Senat in Pinewood's Ballroom*

With the infinitely interesting Charlie Sheen

Tom, Paul, Paula Wagner and Associate Producer Michael Doven

In Prague for 'Mission: Impossible', with Paul, Steve Harding (Production Manager) and Robin Demetriou (First Unit Caterers)

In Red Square with Paramount Pictures VP, Fred Gallo

Phillip Noyce directing 'The Saint'

David Brown (producer), Paul with me behind, Phillip Noyce, Phil Meheux (DoP) and Steve Harding (Production Manager)

Having great fun at a party at the Aerostar with Stefano Priori, who played excellent bass

Me singing my heart out at the big party - when we declared it's all so very boring here

Paul Hitchcock, Steve Harding, Mike Smith and Stefano Priori (Production Accountants) on location in Moscow

The wonderful Chateau Le Vicomte

Shooting 'The Man in the Iron Mask'

Paul's grandson Ben with me and Steve Harding at a premiere (note the champagne!)

'Castaway' with Three T team, Leonid Vereschagin (standing), producer Joan Bradshaw (next to me), and Sergei & Tatiana Gurevich

'Castaway' in Moscow, with my son Martin

*Fox Studios Sydney, the opening party,
where 'Mi2' was one of the first major US movies*

'Mi2' on location in Sydney

'Mi2' rock climbing setup

'Mi2' with Paula Wagner and Paul Hitchcock

'Mi2' car chase which we filmed in Azusa, USA

End of 'Mi2' picture dinner

Working with the lovely Anne Bruning

On my way to 'Mi2' premiere with Beverly Hills hotel manager Vanessa Williams, with whom I negotiated for the unit

A cherished signed photo from Tom Cruise

Sir Anthony Hopkins also gave me a wonderful signed photo

Doyles fish restaurant at Watson Bay Sydney for Sunday lunch with Paula Wagner and Billy Burton (2nd unit director)

The amazing chandelier from Swarovski, provided as product placement and assembled by experts from Austria

One of the many Pinewood backlot exteriors we build for 'Phantom of the Opera'

The 'Fred Claus' PR tour with the crew of our airline

Me with the little people from 'Fred Claus' on the USA publicity tour

We even made it to Hollywood! (L-R) Viktor, Zinaida, Nadezda, Veronika, Natalia, Inna and Alina (interpreter)

In Miami it was 30 degrees and the 'Fred Claus' cast were in their winter clothes!

Allan Cameron (Prod Designer), Anna Sheppard (Costume), Paul and me

Our wedding day in Portugal. (L-R) my grandson Leo (aged 3), daughter in law Rachel, granddaughter Matilda (aged 5), Paul, me and Martin

It was a fairytale wedding day

Full of laughter and fun

Paul's memorial and magnificent redwood tree at Pinewood Studios

CHAPTER 10

Terminal Velocity

Terminal Velocity was a Hollywood Pictures (owned by Disney) action film released in 1994, starring Charlie Sheen, Nastassja Kinski and James Gandolfini. It centred on a daredevil skydiver (Sheen) caught up in a criminal plot by Russian mobsters, who forced him to team up with a secret agent in order to survive.

David Twohy's original spec script was sold to the studio for over $500,000, with Kevin Reynolds and Tom Cruise originally attached as director and star. But other commitments had prevented it.

I boarded for the Moscow element of the shoot as supervising production manager.

The director Deran Sarafian (the nephew of Robert Altman) seemed a bit tired and devoid of much enthusiasm when I met him, which I put down to the fact that it was towards the end of a long shoot. Maybe I should have wondered if there was more to it…?

Nastassja Kinski, meanwhile, was a delight and at that time was partnered with Quincy Jones, who seemed hugely protective of her – overly protective in fact – and when he wasn't around on set, he called her *very* regularly. I know she had been reported as saying she had felt exploited as a young actor, being tricked into appearing in full-frontal nude scenes. She seemed to keep herself very much to herself and didn't socialise with the other cast and crew as a result. Fair enough, I thought, but on one occasion I found myself with her between set-ups and thought that rather than talking about the weather, I'd break the ice by mentioning I'd worked with her father, Klaus Kinski, who had recently passed away. Maybe I expected a fond smile and a few words of reminiscence, but what I got was a shudder as she snapped, 'Don't even say that name to me!' and she moved away.

It wasn't until about five years later, following the revelation that her father had sexually abused her sister Pola, that I read an interview with Nastassja where she stated that whilst he had not molested her as a child, her father had abused her 'in other ways'.

Oh, what a mistake I'd made in bringing his name up!

She was such a sweet lady and true professional, yet she was carrying around that awful childhood trauma.

Charlie Sheen, on the other hand, was problematic in every way.

He'd starred in a number of movies by that point, including the hugely successful *Hot Shots!* in 1991 and had just been awarded his own star on the Hollywood Walk of Fame – so his career was very much on an upward trajectory, as was his ego.

On the eve of shooting, the director and producer held a party at the Aerostar Hotel where we were all staying, but I was busy preparing the call sheet for the following morning and asked my assistant to distribute it, though added I would personally ensure the principals received theirs at the party, as in my experience – and certainly following a party – it had been known for people to 'forget' or even deny they'd ever seen a call sheet.

However, I couldn't find Charlie.

I asked around and was told he was, in fact, in his own suite, throwing his own party. I went along, knocked on his ajar door and discovered just about every hooker in Moscow there.

'Mr Sheen, I have the call sheet for tomorrow,' I told him.

He looked at me quizzically, grabbed the paperwork, crumpled it up and said, 'Call sheet? What call sheet? Don't worry! I will be there!!'

My heart sank.

'Mr Sheen, please read it and make a note of the times…' I pleaded.

'Oh, loosen up, come on in and party!'

I declined his invitation.

Next morning, despite my worst fears, he did turn up on set and on time – albeit a little jaded, and I felt I'd maybe misjudged him and perhaps owed him an apology. However, roll on to day three and I received a phone call from Martin Sheen – Charlie's father – who had specifically asked for me.

'How is he?' Martin Sheen asked.

'Charlie? He's fine,' I replied.

There was a brief pause. 'When is he flying home?'

'Tomorrow. Why?' I enquired.

'Does he have a ticket?'

'Yes…' I replied.

'I specifically asked that he be routed via London to LA is that the case?'

'Yes, Mr Sheen, that is correct.'

'Then can you make sure, please Lidia, that he travels via London…'

'With respect, Mr Sheen,' I answered, 'short of putting him on the plane myself, I will ensure he is driven to the correct terminal at the right time to catch his flight.'

I thought, what am I, his nursemaid?

'Thank you so much. You probably wonder why I'm asking…' Martin Sheen continued.

'It had crossed my mind…'

'Well, Charlie has a problem,' he confided, 'and he could easily fly to Amsterdam to fuel his addiction.'

I then twigged what the call was about and faithfully promised Martin Sheen that I would personally put his son in the car and ensure the driver took him right to the terminal door. With hindsight, I should have asked the driver to see him through check-in and through security.

I went down to the lobby at the hotel at 12pm to meet Charlie and asked if he'd had breakfast or if he wanted a quick lunch, but before he could answer, the hotel manager came running over towards us and demanded I accompany him, all but ignoring Charlie, after first throwing him a withering look.

'What's the problem?' I asked.

'Please. Please come with me,' he beckoned.

I told Charlie I wouldn't be long and would see him in the restaurant, as the manager led me upstairs to Charlie's suite. Once there, he opened the door and revealed absolute carnage – the whole place was trashed, like a bad burglary, with chairs broken, a television thrown at the window, which had smashed, and everything else either upturned or upended. I couldn't believe what I was seeing.

'He will have to pay for everything and cannot leave until he does,' the distraught manager cried.

I went straight to the restaurant, found Charlie and asked him what the hell had happened. He shrugged.

'Charlie, they will not allow you to leave until you pay for all the damage!' I exclaimed. 'You will not be allowed to leave Russia!'

'Ok, Lidia, I'll pay. Let's go to reception now and I'll pay,' he said calmly. Whether this had been a regular occurrence during the production, I don't know, but it would explain why everyone seemed so tired and unmotivated on arriving.

'Charlie, if you didn't like the room, I would have changed it,' I added.

He laughed.

I can't recall how much he was charged, but he put it on his credit card, and I put him into the car and waved him off, feeling totally frustrated.

The next day, Martin Sheen phoned.

'I'm sorry Lidia. I don't blame you, as he would have probably gone there from London anyway. Charlie is in Amsterdam.'

He had changed the ticket at Moscow airport.

I apologised, having given my word, but Martin was terribly kind and understanding. I think it was that understanding and love of his father and family, and a marriage breakdown, that eventually made Charlie realise he couldn't go on like this, and he checked into rehab and turned his life around. It's tragic when such young, talented people go off the rails when success arrives quickly. I truly hope he is now happy and content in his career.

CHAPTER 11

Mission: Impossible

The film rights to the popular 1960s US television series had been owned by Paramount Pictures for many years, but they had failed to come up with a viable big-screen script. That is, until Tom Cruise, who had been a fan of the show since he was young, formed his own production company (in the early 1990s), together with his former agent Paula Wagner. This seemed like the perfect first project.

Tom Cruise had long desired more creative freedom and control over his film projects, and the opportunity to produce – which also meant a bigger share in profits – saw the duo sign a three-year multi-picture financing and distribution deal with Paramount. *Mission: Impossible* was set to be the first off the blocks with a $70 million budget.

Tom personally hired Brian De Palma to direct, after meeting him at a dinner hosted by Steven Spielberg, where he pitched the idea to the director, who, up until that point, was primarily known for dramatic movies. The lure of moving into the action genre proved irresistible to DePalma, and various writers came and went until David Koepp finally rewrote a script by Willard Huyck and Gloria Katz, which had previously ticked most but not quite all of the boxes.

Pre-production commenced at Pinewood in the summer of 1995, reportedly without a finished script. Brian De Palma had meanwhile convinced Cruise to set the first act in Prague, a city rarely seen in contemporary Hollywood movies.

Whilst some elements of the project were in place, it wasn't enough, and with a looming start date, Fred Gallo, the head of production at Paramount, called our office and asked to speak to Paul:

'We've got this film called *Mission: Impossible*, which we've done some preliminary work on, but we will be changing the senior production people we have on it. Tom Cruise is starring and producing, and I'd like you to meet him.'

Of course, Paul was immediately interested but couldn't exactly pop downstairs to their offices at Pinewood to meet Tom and his producing partner, as those 'senior production people' hadn't yet been told they were to be fired.

So, Paul met Paula and Tom in central London, where they explained their Executive Producer – an American gentleman who was in overall charge of budgets, schedules and deals and had clearly been promoted way beyond his ability – would be leaving as 'things were not working out with him'. That's nothing new in this business, of course, where personalities clash and 'creative differences' are often cited, though this particular producer was seemingly out of his depth. He was paid-off, and retired immediately afterwards, I assume with quite a generous severance package.

The project itself was not in a good place, with little to no paperwork or documentation in the Executive Producer's office. It was as though everything had either been trashed or had never existed, but with actors' and key personnel already contracted, any delay would be simply unaffordable for Paramount. Paul needed to move quickly and seemed very excited with the challenge ahead.

I was hugely excited to be involved with such a grand Hollywood adventure too, and had never in my wildest dreams imagined I would be working on a film of this scale and size. Admittedly, being dropped in at the deep end wasn't without its challenges.

There was a large sequence planned to shoot in my home city of Prague, as mentioned, and that was set for early in the new year. Meanwhile, I had planned a big Christmas with friends and family.

Paul said to me, 'You're flying to Prague on December 26th.'
'With all due respect, I don't think so,' I replied.
Paul was taken aback. 'How dare you?' he spluttered.

Before he could say anymore I qualified my earlier statement by explaining that the Czech Republic is largely a Catholic country where everything shuts down for the Christmas holidays, and whilst it might seem a good idea to open up the production office the day after Boxing Day, it would be a pointless and costly exercise as everywhere would be closed, everyone would be off work with their families and I'd be sitting in an office with nothing to do and no one to take my calls – banks, suppliers, government departments for permissions, local co-producers etc. It's the biggest holiday in the country, bar none.

I suggested it would be better if I flew on January 2nd when everyone was back at work and reopened.

To be honest the film was in such a bad place that a week here or there wasn't going to make a huge difference anyway, but Paul was able to use the time between Christmas and New Year to quietly piece together some more of the elements his predecessor had put in place – including a Prague-based co-producer, which was necessary to benefit from the country's film tax incentive. Paul was not at all happy after speaking to them, as they had only ever worked on small films and never an American studio picture, so he suggested Paramount change them for a more experienced outfit. That was easier said than done as the Czech company laughed and said, 'Everything is signed: our deal, the banks we will use, the lawyers, the completion guarantor, etc. are all signed up to OUR production of *Mission: Impossible*.'

Paul checked – there was no mention of Paramount anywhere. The previous Executive Producer had engaged this local company to make the film and given them carte blanche, whilst also making them sole signatories to the bank accounts.

More alarming was the fact that they had arranged 'security' for the production, consisting of armed mercenaries. I was aghast and told the company they were out of their minds – this was a film, not an armed response unit! We just wanted to keep the set secure from petty pilferers and tourists from wandering into frame, and I knew if Tom Cruise had spotted security personnel carrying live weapons, he'd have gone crazy – more than anyone else, he knew how so-called tough guys loved to show off their bravado around him and would probably be very trigger-happy at the slightest provocation.

Again, it showed the company's inexperience and ignorance of working on a large American film, and I made it very clear to them that no one would step onto our set with any sort of weapon if they wanted to avoid an international and diplomatic nightmare. Maybe I wasn't quite so diplomatic myself, but they got the message!

Despite trying, we couldn't change the Prague production outfit – without massive financial consequences – but worse still, Paul then discovered the deals they'd agreed to use certain landmarks and locations were all at astronomically high costs. No sane producer would have agreed to such prices, but they shrugged their shoulders and said their hands were tied by the government, and that was that.

Someone, somewhere, was making a fortune. It stank of corruption.

Paula Wagner was very much a creative sort of producer; in that she liked working on the development and preparation of a project, and that was where her strengths lay. Tom was the type of producer who was always interested in everything, but without ever wanting to get too bogged down with the nitty-gritty of everyday matters; yes, he liked to know all was running to schedule but as he had dialogue to learn, action scenes to choreograph and 'the look' of his character to think about, he didn't have time for much else, so looked to Paul and his Associate Producer Michael Doven to double-check on the finer details.

Paul duly met the local Mayor and explained this was going to be a huge production, unlike anything they'd witnessed before.

'What will it be like when they all arrive?' the Mayor asked arrogantly.

'To be honest, it'll be just like the Russian invasion,' Paul replied, which immediately wiped the grin off the mayor's face.

Our schedule featured mainly night shoots across three square miles of the city, but despite being 'dark', it still needed to be lit enough for the cameras to pick up the action and actors, necessitating generators, lights, trucks and cables – probably more than you've ever seen in your life. In fact, all the American tourists were saying, 'Prague look so wonderful at night and is lit so very beautifully' – thinking it was usual to have everything from the castle to the cathedral, the Charles Bridge and town squares all illuminated brightly. Little did they know it was all due to 'Lee Lighting'! (The British light equipment company).

Director Brian De Palma had selected a number of Government buildings by the river and was quite adamant they were the ones we'd film – and rightly so, as they looked beautiful. But we kept receiving huge facility bills, and each week another would arrive for far more than the previous one. We were about to go over budget unless we were able to renegotiate these ever-increasing fees, but all the officials standing around watching shrugged whenever Paul questioned costs as though they knew nothing about it.

It was then I suggested to Paul – either in a moment of madness or sheer genius – that I would try to set a meeting up with the President of the country, Václav Havel, who I knew was a great lover of the arts. I duly explained to the President's office that we were thrilled to be filming in Prague but were encountering a few problems and wondered if he would consent to meeting the producers... and Tom Cruise.

He readily agreed to meet us – who wouldn't want to meet Tom Cruise?

Tom, Paula, Paul, and I headed to the castle along with Jon Voight (who tagged along as he wanted to meet the President), plus an interpreter – an independent person to make sure nothing was missed, or rather misstated. A nice lady met us there. She was polite but very businesslike.

'Who are you?' I asked curtly.

I then realised she was Olga Havel, the President's wife, who had obviously been sent to pay us lip service and offer the President's warm wishes – before getting rid of us. I quickly tried to cover my mistake.

'Oh, may I say how much more beautiful you are in person, compared to your photographs,' I grovelled.

Paul looked at me, a little puzzled.

'Every picture of you… they just don't do you justice,' I added, to further ingratiate myself and buy us a little time before being thrown out.

She then saw Tom Cruise, who said he was honoured to meet her, and as the flattery grew, she began to thaw and eventually ushered this charming Hollywood contingent through to meet her husband, who in turn seemed curious as to why his wife hadn't sent us on our way.

We swiftly explained that we were thoroughly enjoying being in the capital city, and how it looked magnificent on the big screen, but then mentioned the bills the Ministry was sending each week.

Havel said, 'I'm delighted you're enjoying yourselves here, but there really isn't a lot I can do.'

'But you are the President!' I exclaimed.

He thought for a moment, looked at Tom Cruise, who smiled warmly at him, and then started chatting, taking a genuine interest in what our plans were, the locations we were using, the stunts and so on, before asking Paul, 'So, what exactly do you want me to do?'

Paul queried if there was any way he could help reduce the facility bills we were receiving.

'No, I can't,' he replied.

'How come?' Paul asked.

'My hands are tied. I may be President, but it is the Prime Minister and his government who set the laws and rules, and I cannot overturn their decisions,' he shrugged.

I was getting more and more pissed off, not helped by sleep deprivation associated with filming nights, and heard myself saying 'Well, Mr President, you are obviously only a puppet!' and with that I ushered my colleagues out.

Whether he had a word with the Prime Minister I don't know, but the bills were a little less outrageous in the two weeks we had left in Prague, including filming in the Old Town Square for the dramatic sequence where Ethan Hunt (Tom Cruise) was in a restaurant and a giant aquarium exploded… well part of it was shot there, as The Akvárium restaurant exterior was built on the studio set in order we had total control over the explosions and flooding. By the way, the fish – when it exploded – were fake, but movie regulations state that whenever animals are involved in American movies that a representative from the American Humane Society must be present. A 'fish specialist' duly arrived and was paid a day's salary to watch a tank full of rubber amphibians float around. Not bad work if you can get it.

There were 16 tonnes of water in those tanks, and some concern was raised that when they were detonated, a lot of glass would fly around and might endanger our leading man, so Brian De Palma tried the sequence with a stuntman, but felt it didn't look convincing, so he asked Tom if he would do it. Of course, Tom readily agreed and emerged unscathed.

Towards the end of our time in Prague, I must admit that I started looking over my shoulder, fearful I'd overstepped the mark with the President – and remember it was only a few years after the fall of communism and I'd known all too well what it was like to be suspected as a collaborator of the West. I wondered if I'd be allowed to leave the airport with the rest of the cast and crew, or if I would be detained, so I mentioned my worries to Paul, that having insulted the President, I may be a marked woman.

'Well, goodbye to you. What else can I say – you really should have kept your mouth shut,' Paul replied with a wry smile.

I know he was right, but I had hoped for a few reassuring words of comfort!

As it happened, everything went smoothly, luckily, and we all flew back to London without a hitch or a hand on my shoulder. I had certainly learned a valuable lesson.

On returning to Pinewood to shoot the interiors, the climax of the story was set on a train going into the Channel Tunnel (which was constructed inside the huge 007 Stage at the studio) with our hero on top. Paul arranged a meeting with Eurostar to discuss collaborating and possible promotional tie-ins, but they didn't want to know – they were not remotely interested in cooperating, fearing it might put people off travelling through the recently opened undersea railway if it was portrayed as a terrorist target in a major movie.

Feeling we were facing a bit of a problem, Paul flew to Paris to meet the Sales & Marketing Executive at TGV, who was wonderful, immediately saw the PR opportunities and willingly arranged for us to have all the trains and rolling stock we needed.

To achieve the effect of Tom clinging to the roof of a fast-moving train on the stage, we brought in loads of wind machines, essentially aeroplane engines, which pushed huge amounts of air around with great force. Tom wanted to do his own stunts and really didn't want any safety wires attached, which worried a lot of people on set.

'What'll happen if I don't wear the wires?' he asked Paul.

'You'll be at Shepperton, and we'll be at Pinewood!' Paul answered candidly.

It was a tough sequence, and although it was mainly set against a green screen, the force of the 140-mph wind hitting Tom distorted his face and pushed him off balance several times, meaning the safety wires did indeed save him from being catapulted through the stage's roof. They were later 'painted out' in post-production, so nobody knew they'd been there.

The film was so full of terrific and stylish sequences, and of course, everyone remembers the sequence where Tom infiltrates a vault, drops down from a rope horizontally and hangs just inches above his target. His fitness and stamina were enviable. He really reinvented the action movie genre, and key to its success was Brian De Palma, who brought dramatic tension to the movie.

Interestingly, before we started shooting, Paramount insisted that the revised budget and schedule Paul put together was signed off not only by Cruise, Wagner and our accountant Mike Smith, but by the director too. However, one signature was missing as we moved into production – Brian's.

Paul approached him one day early on.

'Brian, I'm sorry to raise it but I'm being really beaten up by the studio over getting you to sign off.'

'Where is it?' he asked.

'It's with your assistant in the office.'

'OK,' Brian replied.

A couple of days went by, and he still hadn't signed the paperwork, so Paul approached him again.

'Brian, I know you have more important things to worry about than this, but is there a problem with the schedule or budget that you don't want to commit to?'

'I don't want to sign it,' he replied.

'Can I ask why?' Paul asked, with growing frustration.

'The reason, Paul, is because Paramount have not signed my contract, so why should I sign this?'

Paul returned the paperwork to Paramount... and it remained unsigned.

In any other business, contracts would have to be signed before a job commences – but not in movies!

Brian was always on set early and worked very hard, but when we broke for lunch around 1pm you wouldn't see him back on set until 3pm, because he used to like to have a little rest. Quite often, we'd run through quite late into the evenings, so everyone understood why he needed 40 winks. One lunchtime, Tom wanted to get something or other underway earlier and went looking for Brian.

'Mr De Palma is having a lie down and will be ready at 3pm,' his assistant said.

Tom was about to argue, and Paul stepped in to say, 'Tom, it's the same every day. This is how he works; we'll just have to wait.'

I can't say I had much personal experience of Brian De Palma, as even though we were on the same picture for months, I don't think he ever spoke directly to me. I guess I was just a minion, but of course, I was there behind Paul every step of the way to deal with the various requests and whims that came our way.

For example, the final shot of the movie was to be filmed on a Tuesday, at Heathrow Airport, where Tom's character says goodbye to Ving Rhames' and the film ends. On the Sunday evening prior, Brian called Paul at home.

'Paul, I don't want to shoot at Heathrow.'

'Why not Brian?'

'It doesn't work, it doesn't work for me,' he replied.

'But we film on Tuesday... what is it you're looking to do instead?'

'I want to shoot in the courtyard of a pub overlooking St Paul's Cathedral,' the director concluded.

Paul called me and told me their conversation ended with him thinking, 'How the hell are we going to pull this one off in 24 hours?'

He asked that I call Chris Brock – our location manager – and a couple of others, and they then tore about London on the Monday, and mercifully by the late afternoon were able to take Brian to see a pub that they'd found. He said he was 'very happy'.

Paul and I, meanwhile, tracked down the owner, Lord somebody or other, who lived in Manchester. After apologising for the late-evening intrusion, Paul explained, 'I'm from Paramount Pictures, and we are producing a film called *Mission: Impossible* with Tom Cruise, and I'm a very desperate man.'

'Mr Hitchcock,' he replied, 'nothing gives me more pleasure than talking to a desperate man.'

'Oh?' Paul queried.

'Because there is no room for negotiation!'

Paul reached an agreement, and with a small crew, they filmed right in the centre of London City the next morning, and Brian was very appreciative.

Incidentally, a couple of years later, MGM called the office and said they were going to make a film with Brian De Palma called *Nazi Gold*, which, as the title suggests, was all about the gold snaffled away by Hitler in Swiss Banks, and this story was about the raid to reclaim it.

'Would you be interested?' they asked.

Paul thought it sounded fun and so gave Brian a call to discuss it all, though tracking him down was a tricky exercise in itself, as you never knew if he was in the Hamptons, in New York City, LA or anywhere else for that matter, as he never stayed in one place very long. Finally, we received word he was staying at Shutters Hotel in Santa Monica, California. Paul phoned and said MGM had asked him to make contact.

'I'll send you the script,' Brian said, ever a man of few words.

'Well, would it be okay for me to work on the film with you?' Paul asked.

'Yes, sure,' he answered. 'Read the script and just move on, look for locations.'

'Shouldn't we meet though?' Paul asked.

'Paul. You know what I look like, and I know what you look like. Why do we need to meet?'

MGM wanted to start shooting in the summer, so Paul and I headed off to Zurich and Geneva in the spring and kept sending ideas and reports back to Brian.

We spent around three weeks in Switzerland and must admit we were met rather frostily by all the banks, as they operated under tight veils of secrecy, of course, but eventually we made some headway. However, we hadn't heard anything back from Brian. When Paul called the MGM office, they told him, 'Oh, he resigned from the picture a week ago.'

'But we've been traipsing around Europe and have just sent him another bundle of papers and photos,' Paul said, feeling rather exasperated.

We never heard another word from Brian until another film came along almost ten years later – *The Black Dahlia* – for which independent finance had been raised on a relatively modest budget, away from the studio system, which the director was then seemingly rallying against. Paul didn't think it was a project that would work on the budget and timescale they had in mind, so he declined to be involved.

I was thrilled to be invited to the premiere of *Mission: Impossible* by Tom Cruise personally, in both LA and London. It was honestly the highlight of my career, and both were huge events. In LA, I was put up in a wonderful five-star hotel, with a limousine at my disposal – and thought I'd arrived… finally, the girl from Prague was in Hollywood!

The London premiere was in Leicester Square and was followed by a huge party on the top floor in Harrods, where the most glorious food and champagne flowed freely.

The film was pure entertainment from start to finish, and the reactions at the premieres were wonderful.

I realise the plot was a little convoluted in parts, and amusingly, just after the closing titles ran, we were standing in the foyer of the Odeon when two ladies came out of the loo and the first one said, 'I really enjoyed that, but what was it about?'

The second said, 'I've no idea, but wasn't it good?'

Incidentally, and most importantly, the film was delivered on time and under budget – a rarity in Hollywood – and on its release in May 1996 it grossed almost half a billion dollars against an $80 million budget. Paul Hitchcock was widely congratulated for turning what was initially a troubled production into one of the most successful box office hits of the year.

Consequently, there was some discussion about a franchise, and I remember Tom saying, 'Well, if it does develop into a series, there will only be three. No more than three.'

Famous last words, eh?

Oh, I should mention that because the movie was quite demanding on all our time, we didn't really socialise very much – we didn't have the time to – with other crew members, though Paul and I became friendly with Chris Soldo, our wonderful First Assistant Director, and stayed in touch forevermore.

A consequence of this friendship was that Chris knew we both loved Tony Bennett, who Chris' father was a musician and arranger for, and in 2004 invited us to the Walt Disney Concert Hall of downtown Los Angeles to attend one of Bennett's concerts. What's more, Chris arranged for us to meet the great man afterwards. When Tony commented on my accent and wanted to know more about which part of Prague I was from, I was genuinely taken aback that he took such an interest in me, though I felt the eyes of the people behind burning into my back, obviously thinking I was hogging and boring the maestro! I didn't have a picture or even a programme to sign, but Chris later arranged for a wonderful, signed photo.

Chris came to our wedding in Portugal in 2012 and then 10 years later to our 'tin' wedding anniversary party, and in 2016 arranged for us to attend another fantastic concert, this time with Lady Gaga in New York Radio City. It's great to know somebody well connected, and all as a result of *Mission: Impossible*!

CHAPTER 12

The Saint

Without doubt, *The Saint* was one of the craziest productions I have ever been involved in.

Paul Hitchcock had gained a reputation for rescuing troubled productions, and *The Saint* became another of those.

The studio (Paramount) had appointed Branko Lustig as production manager and had shipped him out to Moscow to head up pre-production on the project. Unfortunately, rumours were abound of progress being slow, it becoming too expensive, and Branko had seemingly engaged a lot of people from Croatia in order to get 'cheap labour', but they all proved to be totally out of their depth. Added to this, the original producer Robert Evans had walked off the project – though contractually still retained a producer credit – and the Executive Producer Robert S Baker (who had made the earlier TV series and retained some of the screen rights), seemed to have no day-to-day involvement yet contractually retained a credit too. They, along with Roger Moore, who (contractually) didn't get an on-screen credit but ironically did receive a fee for producing and starring – neither of which he ended up doing but still banked the cheque – added to the number of producers who were not actually involved in doing anything. Before a single frame of film had been shot, there was already quite a checkered production history on the project.

The film had, in fact, been in development for a decade and went through many rewrites. Following Robert Evans' departure, veteran producer David Brown came on board along with director Phillip Noyce. Other producers appointed included William J MacDonald (who was a partner with Robert Evans in his company) and Mace Neufield – nowadays there seem to be more producers than stars, don't you think?

David Brown was an absolute gentleman, very much of the old school, and he'd made some terrific films ranging from *The Sting* to *Jaws* and *Driving Miss Daisy*. He was highly respected and well-liked. My abiding memory of David was that at 11am every single day, no matter where we were in the world, he'd call his wife Helen (who was the editor-in-chief of Cosmopolitan magazine for 32 years), for no particular reason other than just to see how she was, what was happening during the hours ahead, and to wish her a lovely day. It was so touching and actually made me realise I didn't call my son nearly often enough!

Mace Neufield was a very successful and respected producer of films such as *The Omen*, *The Hunt For Red October* and *Patriot Games* – so was an assured pair of hands. He was more on the creative side of things, dealing with the stars, the writers, etc. and when you have big personalities you need a confident, creative producer to handle them.

Both David and Mace were on set throughout the production every day. I didn't have many (if any) dealings with William J MacDonald, but then again, I think he was concerned with the financial side of the project.

My involvement came about when Fred Gallo (of Paramount) called Paul to ask if he could spare me to work with him in Moscow, for a short time, whilst he tried to 'sort out a mess'.

He duly arrived at Paul's office at Pinewood to chat, and the next day I flew with Fred to Russia, not really knowing much about what 'mess' it was exactly, nor my role.

'Lidia,' he said to me at Heathrow airport, 'I don't talk on planes... I don't want to talk... I'm tired... I have jet lag, so I will tell you your role once we land.'

That made me feel even more anxious than I already was; it's intimidating enough being with the head honcho of a studio who is en route to sort out a troubled film, let alone without knowing why you're actually there!

On landing, the local Russian production service company we'd engaged, Three T, who were amazingly efficient and brilliant, organised a presidential-style motorcade to take us from the airport to the hotel with police escorts and outriders. Fred was hugely embarrassed and went berserk – he was hoping to arrive without any great fuss to quietly find out why things were so troubled.

'I don't want all this!' Fred protested.

I told him I'd take care of it for the future and placated him a little by explaining it was customary for them to honour important visiting dignitaries, but also that although it was only 45 minutes' drive from the airport, the roads in the city were constantly jammed with the most horrendous traffic – much worse than Los Angeles – and this was to ensure we didn't get held up.

'Okay, okay,' he said, feeling less on edge.

When we reached the hotel, Fred said that he wanted to unpack and would call my room in thirty minutes – I still had no idea why I was there. When the call eventually came, he explained in a polite but very businesslike manner:

'This is how it will work. I know you speak fluent Russian, but you will just listen. I don't want them to know you speak their language. You will sit in on my meetings, and then at the end of the day, I will call you and you will tell me everything that was said. I don't trust their translators.'

We had meetings with the local police, government officials, the army, customs officers and so on, and all accompanied by the state-appointed translators. The meetings had all been set up by Branko Lustig, who had claimed to Fred that there was Russian mafia interference going on with corruption at every turn, and that there weren't even any half-decent hotels anywhere in Moscow. In short, he painted a pretty bad picture to the head of the studio and furthermore claimed that the whole crew, including the main actors, would have to be housed in communist run hotels, which were akin to prisons with poor food and with soldiers on sentry duty outside.

I remember thinking to myself, 'Bullshit!' as I knew of the National, Metropolitan and Kempinski hotels, which were beautiful – and those were just off the top of my head. I couldn't quite understand why Lustig was saying all this negative stuff and what he was hoping to achieve.

That evening, Fred phoned my room for his briefing, and I started by explaining about the beautiful international hotels where there were great restaurants, and whilst I agreed there might be some corruption, I added that it existed everywhere I've ever filmed, including in LA and London.

'What Lustig is saying is simply not true,' I concluded.

After three days of meetings I flew back with Fred to London and on the plane – he did want to chat this time – he said, 'We are in pre-production, the film is greenlit, contracts have been signed, we have our stars and our director – but what we don't have is an Executive Producer I can trust to run the nuts-and-bolts of the production and report back to us daily and truthfully about budget and scheduling matters.'

There was a pause.

I said, 'Um, okay?'

'Lidia, who do you think should take on that role?' he asked.

I felt it was a loaded question, as he and Paul went back many years and he knew exactly how skilled Paul was in turning troubled productions around.

'There's only one person, Fred, and you know him well,' I replied.

On landing at Heathrow, we called Paul to meet with Fred and he was offered the movie.

Various high-profile actors had been offered the lead but had passed for one reason or another, until the studio announced Val Kilmer and Elizabeth Shue had been signed. To be honest, they had about as much chemistry as me and the secret police back in Prague.

I set about organising accommodation with the luxurious Kempinski. There were some very nice suites for the lead actors, along with Mace Neufeld, who was accompanied by his then partner, who insisted that he had to have a grand white piano in his suite. That wasn't possible, but the hotel provided a small (though not white) piano in his room whilst saying he could have exclusive access to the grand piano in the lobby. So, everybody was happy – and who do you think had to organise all of this? Me, of course! It wasn't just the stars who had a list of demands.

On the flip side, one of our local coordinators was an American girl named Ellen who lived in Moscow and had done for some years. She suggested that she'd like to cook a meal for some of us in the main unit at her apartment. We all thought yes, that sounded great as, whilst we had access to a fairly decent restaurant, during pre-production you have to pay for your own meals – there are no dinners nor expenses – so coupled with Moscow being very expensive, we all agreed there's nothing ever like home cooking. We were a bit of a motley crew in the early days on the picture, and I think I may have been the only one who had been to Russia before, so it was a lovely opportunity for everyone to see the real country.

Ellen told me she found Moscow so fresh and so different to the West, but I wasn't so sure personally. I wondered if she was a bit of a communist at heart, but nevertheless, one Friday, four of us headed to her apartment with great enthusiasm and knocked on the door only to be welcomed into the tiniest little room with everything crammed in – kitchenette, lounge, shower – along with a single solitary light bulb dangling, shaded with a newspaper that had been crafted into a sort of spherical shape.

'Ellen, you're American and yet you enjoy this lifestyle?' I asked, less than diplomatically.

'I love it,' she replied although I wondered who she was trying to convince.

The crew all looked at each other as we sat with a plate on our laps, perched on chairs muttering pleasantries about how nice it was to be there.

***

Thanks to Three T's recommendation, the majority of cast and crew stayed at Aerostar, which was a Canadian-Russian owned modern 9-storey business hotel with very spacious rooms on Leningradsky Prospekt. The food served there was flown in from either Europe or Canada and was exquisite.

When I initially went to do the deal with the Canadian manager of the hotel, I said I needed 150 rooms and 'this is my budget'. He took a look at the number I'd written down and said 'no'. He added, 'I can sell these rooms at twice the price you're asking. Yes, I can do a little bit of a discount, but nothing like what you're asking for.'

'I think you're making a mistake,' I countered, ' because I can tell you now that the 200 crew will be sitting here in your bar every night spending their per diems, because there's nowhere else around here for them to go.'

The Aerostar wasn't in the centre of Moscow, it was maybe 15 minutes' drive from Red Square, and that would mean taking the Metro or cabs, but the manager wasn't convinced, 'They will all go into central Moscow.'

'Yes,' I agreed, 'they will. But only in the first week. After their initial fascination, they'll discover it's not so convenient, the Metro closes at 11pm and they're missing out on valuable drinking time.'

'OK,' the manager agreed, 'what we'll do is agree to 10 days on your budget, but if they don't spend what you're suggesting, then we revert to my deal. Is that agreed?'

We shook hands. And who do you think was right?!

During the first week on location, all the crew got changed after shooting and went out into the city... only to start complaining, 'Oh it's such a drag, we have to count the stops on the Metro because it's all written in Russian' and that it was 'so bitterly cold out there'.

They looked around the American themed bar in the hotel, the wonderful Western food on the menus, and all agreed it was a lovely and familiar place to spend their evenings in the warmth amongst friends.

They duly drank the place dry.

There was a terrible accident during pre-production when our casting director Elisabeth Leustig was returning from dinner at a restaurant one evening (totally sober, I should add) and was hit by a car on the road directly outside where she was crossing. The driver didn't stop – nor was he ever found – and Elisabeth tragically died at the scene. As I previously mentioned, the traffic in Moscow is terrible and a lot of the drivers there are pretty bad ones. It was a huge shock to us all, and the film is dedicated to her memory.

I know it may sound cold-hearted, but in the film world there is little time for sentiment, with the clock ticking and the dollar signs rolling over. A call was placed to London and enquiries were made. Casting director Patsy Pollock was available and a couple of days later she arrived in Moscow. It's never nice having to replace someone else on a film, not least in such difficult and sad circumstances, but Patsy put on a brave face and set to work. It was only later we discovered that Patsy's house had been broken into earlier that day when she was called, and along with dealing with that and the shock news of Elisabeth, she was able to pack her bags and travel – she was so very highly professional, for which we were all incredibly grateful.

***

When Val Kilmer arrived from LA he introduced us to his new assistant, saying that everything involving him had to go via her.

We discovered that he'd recently met her at a downtown florist shop she was working in. She had no idea about being on a film set, and in fact no idea about being a personal assistant to anyone.

Val said he wanted a few days to recover from the jet lag and to acclimatise, and basically didn't want to be bothered.

I attempted to meet with her but could never find the woman – she was never in the office or hotel room. Invariably, she was in the gym working out – she did so many workouts I could have been forgiven for assuming she was training for the next Olympics.

Phillip Noyce wanted to talk with all the lead actors together one morning and asked that I call everyone, but again, I couldn't find her and ended up traipsing down to the gym. I was so frustrated by this point that I shouted at her, 'There is an important meeting with the director who wants Val to attend.'

'Val isn't to be disturbed today,' she squeaked before carrying on running on the treadmill.

'Listen, you go and knock on his door and tell him his director wants to talk to him,' I snapped.

She did, and the meeting went ahead. Afterwards, Val appeared and I asked if I could have a word with him. In a very laidback manner, he said, 'Sure you can,' and I laid it on the line.

'Val, you do not have an assistant. You have a gym buddy. I cannot communicate with her, and even when I eventually locate her, she is not interested in the job or you.'

'She is always in the gym, you say?' he asked.

'Yes!' I replied.

'So, what do you suggest?' he queried.

'I suggest you get rid of her and we get you a proper assistant who knows what the job entails and knows what is required.'

'Okay,' he agreed, 'but can I meet her first?'

Sallie Hard, an experienced assistant, flew in from London the next day and just as she landed in Moscow, the florist flew out.

Val had just divorced his wife, Joanne Whalley and was now involved with Cindy Crawford, who in turn had recently divorced her husband, Richard Gere; in fact, I remember her flying in to Pinewood during the shoot of *First Knight* to visit Richard, and they seemed so much in love.

There was quite a buzz within the production office that Cindy Crawford, who was at the height of her fame and popularity, was coming over to Moscow and that they were arranging her flight tickets, and they asked who could meet her at the airport… they looked at me.

A year or two earlier, during one of the quiet spells in the industry, Paul Hitchcock had asked me if I maybe had ideas for an alternative career should things not pick up. I said yes, I rather fancied I'd make a good diplomat. Well, after spitting out his coffee, Paul almost wet himself laughing, saying if there was anyone more undiplomatic than me, he'd yet to meet them. So, I think he probably raised an eyebrow when he heard I was heading off to meet Miss Crawford, worried I might put my foot in it.

I arrived at Sheremetyevo International Airport to welcome our VIP guest, who insisted I call her Cindy, and I found her to be so gracious and down to earth that it probably gave me the courage to ask, once we were in the car, whatever made her divorce Richard Gere, as they seemed such a perfect couple. It was lucky Paul wasn't in the car with us, as he'd have likely had a fit that I'd been so forthright and – in his eyes – probably inappropriate to our leading man's girlfriend.

Cindy thought for a moment and replied, 'That's a rather personal question which I'm not going to answer, but what I will say is "differences and ego", and I wanted to act, but Richard said, "no way".'

I was going to ask why she would then take up with another actor who probably shared the same view, but bit my lip.

She was an absolute darling, who was fascinated by history, and she visited so many of the museums, galleries and palaces whilst in Moscow. Towards the end of the shoot, I asked her what travel arrangements she'd like the production to make for her, but she told me not to worry as she had a job with Coca-Cola and they'd offered to send a private jet. I smiled and said, 'How the other half live, eh?' and she gave a little giggle and said it would save the film a few dollars.

I missed her when she left, as did everyone else as she was truly lovely – though I must admit she made us all feel a bit inferior when she walked on set every day looking a million dollars even in an old pair of jeans and t-shirt, while some of the people who'd been in hair and make-up for hours simply faded into the background!

***

Meanwhile, after four weeks, the hotel manager at the Aerostar said that because we were spending so much money, he wanted to throw a party for us with *everyone* from the production company invited!

On the night, Paul exclaimed he'd never seen such large bowls of caviar in his life, and there was so much champagne flowing that it must have caused a national shortage in France. The function suite was festooned with decorations and literally dripped with decadence. Oh, there was a band playing live music too, and many Russian dignitaries came as guests.

Now, we had been grumbling to the main office back in London that during the day, the lunch offerings from the unit caterers were poor, that it was biting cold all the time, and generally it was a very tough place to film. Added to that, we were running short of film stock. It was quite a picture of woe we'd unwittingly painted, to be honest.

Paul requested that a member of the production team from London brought the new shipment of 35mm film stock personally, as he didn't trust courier companies and it was vitally important that it arrived on time in order that any shooting days were not wasted. An assistant named Hazel duly arrived with the stock, and having been told about the terrible food and tough conditions we were working under, she'd obviously arrived with some preconceived ideas about what to expect. On arriving, she asked at the front desk to put a call through to my room, but there was no answer, so she enquired if anyone knew where I was, as it was really quite urgent that I took the delivery. After a bit of mumbling and chatting behind the desk someone said yes, they knew where I was and offered to take her up to the function suite where someone opened the door to reveal Hazel clutching two cans of film stock, with her mouth wide open in shock as she surveyed the scene before her – everyone was completely legless, and I was sitting on top of a large piano with two Russian generals either side of me, wearing one of their hats on my head, complete with a large cigar in my mouth whilst at the same time conducting the band with a makeshift baton.

Hazel's first words were, 'Ah! So, this is how bad it is?'

What a first impression!

We dragged Hazel in to join us, and I must admit, despite the tough conditions, we had great fun during the shoot in Moscow. I say tough, and by that I mean minus 25 degrees temperature at night, and we had to bring in heaters to warm up the dolly-tracks that the cameras ran along, as they'd frozen solid.

One day, filming in Red Square, there were hundreds and hundreds of extras, whom we had to cater for, and while the main unit was catered for by First Unit Caterers, headed by Robin Demetriou, for the extras, I recommended a Czech company who came in and prepared some good, tasty meals at a decent price. We were so happy with them, in fact, that they also came back with us to London to do the same.

After the main unit returned to Pinewood, I stayed behind to oversee the wrap of everything, which Paul wanted supervised and said he could spare me, but I must admit, once everyone else had shipped out, I did feel somewhat isolated. There were only a handful of us Western crew at the Aerostar, and we no longer enjoyed special catering or parties either. But once a week, my little indulgence was to head to the Kempinski for a cappuccino!

***

Back in London, with production in full swing, there was great secrecy surrounding Volvo introducing their latest model, the C70, on screen with the film. The company had a long association with *The Saint*, going back to Roger Moore's days, and undoubtedly paid a fair few dollars for the privilege.

On set in Oxford, the car arrived completely covered over on a low-loader, and such was the security that the cover was only allowed to come off for the scene and then had to go straight back on. Everyone was sworn to secrecy and cameras were banned from the set that day, but would you believe that some paparazzi actually went to the lengths of paying locals whose apartments and homes overlooked where we were shooting, to move out, into luxury hotels, whilst they set up cameras with long lenses to get the shots they wanted, and images of the hush-hush C70 appeared in newspapers.

I realised the lengths some photographers will go to, and it wasn't a pleasant feeling.

In other technological advances, Simon Templar uses a Nokia 9000 Communicator mobile phone, which was cutting-edge when it was introduced in 1996, functioning as both a handheld phone and a clamshell pocket computer, complete with a mini keyboard and several built-in apps. Again, the production received some funds to feature the product.

In the original script, the heroine, Dr Emma Russell, played by Elizabeth Shue, died. She was poisoned.

When the film was completed, it was first shown to the heads of Paramount Pictures in LA, who all came out of the screening room applauding Phillip Noyce, who they dubbed 'the new David Lean'. They told Paul he was himself a saint and their good omen. You can imagine that for us to receive such effusive praise from these seasoned veterans and movie moguls was humbling, and that evening we hit the town – Paul, myself, Terry Rawlings (our editor), Steve Harding (our line producer), Phillip Noyce and a couple of others – and celebrated hard, thinking that we'd made our masterpiece. This was really the dawn of greater things.

The next day, the film was put out to test audiences – office workers, cleaners, manual workers, newsagents etc – who were quite often dragged in off the street without even being questioned whether they liked movies, had seen any other recently or even if they had decent eyesight. Their opinion, it would seem, on what is a good film is more significant than film-makers, studio executives and seasoned professionals. Consequently, we were all hauled into Sherry Lansing's office at Paramount where, 24 hours on from declaring the team geniuses, she proceeded to tear a strip off us all for delivering a film with 'the worst test scores in ten years'.

We were so deflated and thought that was that, none of us would work ever again.

Paul asked what the scoring suggested: the ending was the main problem they said – the 'experts' felt the heroine, Dr Russell, shouldn't die, so that meant rewrites and reshoots were called for.

There were two rounds of re-shoots, both in the UK, with the first taking place over 8 days in December 1996, ending just before Christmas, and the second over another 8 days in Oxford, during January 1997. They ended up costing over $2 million. Val Kilmer initially refused to return but, with many pretty tough conditions and a hefty fee, eventually agreed. I guess we all have our price. I should add he worked very hard, seven days a week, when he did arrive.

Ironically the new ending did nothing to improve the film and in my humble opinion I think it worked better as initially written, because the impact of the heroine dying was pretty significant with her collapsing in The Saint's arms (having been poisoned) and the final reel sees Templar set out to destroy the villains' plans and avenge her death, all culminating in a tense action sequence in a stairwell, which is disintegrating around them, where the duo end up on a huge chandelier suspended above blazing oil into which the bad guy plummets to a fiery death. It was pretty tense stuff.

It then had Templar returning to Dr. Russell's home, where he finds a letter from her, and with a tear in his eye he vows from now on to use his skills only for good. To my mind, that was a strong ending motivated by revenge, but then setting our hero onto an important path for future adventures.

If you watch carefully, footage from the original ending features in the first trailer. Phillip Noyce said he hopes one day to be able to restore the original version for DVD.

Following the reshoots, the release date and premiere were locked in for April 19th. I remember after the premiere, Phillip Noyce invited Paul and me to a big garden party in LA.

'Phillip, how can you guarantee it'll be good weather?' I asked curiously.

'Because I live in LA, it's always nice weather,' he replied matter-of-factly. He was correct of course, it was.

Reviews were mixed, and box-office returns on the $70million picture were decent at $170 million, but when you think that same year *Jurassic Park: The Lost World* took $618million, the Bond film grossed $340million and *Air Force One* took $315million it puts it in perspective as being a bit of a misfire.

But I have to say it was a very interesting 7 or 8 months of my life.

CHAPTER 13

The Man In The Iron Mask

MGM's Production Chief, Bob Relyea, phoned to speak to Paul, saying it was urgent. I explained he was in Portugal on holiday, but gave him the villa number knowing Paul would be keen to take an urgent enquiry.

'Are you currently on a movie?' he asked.

Paul answered that he was taking a break, but no, he didn't have anything on.

'I'll call you back tomorrow,' Bob said, and hung up.

The phone rang late the following evening:

'Paul. We're delighted you're free. Can you be in Paris on Monday?'

Never one to say no until he'd heard through the proposition, Paul said he could drive back home, then hop over to Paris. He had barely been at his villa 24 hours.

'What's the film?' Paul enquired.

'The Man in The Iron Mask.'

'Hang on,' Paul replied, 'that's already shooting.'

Bob Relyea explained the producer was about to be fired as the project was in trouble. It seemed Paul was developing a reputation for rescuing films, though the worry with a picture already shooting is that the crew don't take kindly to being told 'you've been doing it all wrong and I'm taking over'. On the earlier movies that Paul had taken over they hadn't actually rolled cameras, so it was a slightly different proposition, and for that reason, Paul was a little hesitant. But following a brief discussion about the fee on offer, he thought to himself that Paris is a very pleasant place to work, so why not?

Paul asked that I book him the flights and that I, along with his long-time friend and line producer Steve Harding, flew in a week later. I asked how long we were likely to be there, only for Paul to reply, 'You'd best book an open return. It'll be three to four months at least.'

Fortunately, we had a great logistics agency at Pinewood, The Travel Company, and they'd worked on so many films that they knew all the vagaries and uncertainties presented by productions, including the frequent last-minute changes of plans, whilst also being mindful of keeping costs down. I spoke to Mike, the owner, and asked him to dedicate a staff member exclusively to us so I wouldn't have to explain to different people each time I called who I was, where we were and what the film was etc. Sue Roberts was assigned to our show and asked me, 'How long do you expect to be in Paris?'

'Twelve to sixteen weeks,' I replied.

'Oh, how very boring for you,' she jokingly laughed. We immediately clicked, and I knew she was on my wavelength so that was one less worry straight away.

The film had a great cast, including Jeremy Irons, Gerard Depardieu, John Malkovich, Gabriel Byrne and a young Leonardo DiCaprio in two roles – King Louis XIV and a prisoner whose identity was literally masked because he was believed to be the older, illegitimate brother of Louis XIV who could have contested the right to the French throne. It was all good, rousing stuff.

***

I arranged a hotel for Paul, Steve Harding and myself away from the rest of the crew as Paul felt we were already invading the production so wanted us to be slightly detached from everyone else at night whilst a plan of action was formulated, primarily to avoid any unpleasant run-ins or challenge to allegiances.

A small, privately owned boutique hotel on the Left Bank was recommended, with just ten rooms, and I must say it looked very characterful. On arriving with many large suitcases, I asked for a porter.

'Porter? Porter? We don't have one,' the receptionist shrugged in a typically Gallic way.

'How am I supposed to move all these bags?' I asked.

'That's up to you,' she replied.

Charming, I thought. Welcome to Paris!

The luggage was the least of our worries though, as when we arrived at the studio the following Monday, we realised MGM hadn't told the producer he'd actually been fired, as he was standing on the stage asking what Paul was doing there.

Can you imagine the huge embarrassment? Here was Paul, parachuted in to help first-time director Randall Wallace (who'd earlier won an Oscar nomination for writing *Braveheart*) on a big-budget movie with perhaps the biggest star of the day – fresh from his success with *Titanic* – and an inept producer whose every decision to date had proven to be a bad one, making Paul look like the bad guy!

Paul called MGM and told them that they needed to do their own dirty work, and of course, word swiftly spread around set about what was happening. The French crew immediately called a strike, saying they didn't want the original producer to leave. Paul knew he risked a mutiny if he stated the picture was massively over-schedule and budget just two weeks after starting, but the situation wasn't helped by Jeremy Irons' makeup lady saying in front of everyone, 'He was doing a fine job. He's a lovely man to work with and everything is going fine.'

Paul became very irritated and snapped, 'I think it would be much better if you concentrated on Jeremy's make-up and let me decide just how fine this picture is, because I don't think you're in any position to make such a comment.'

Well, that was it. The whole crew fell silent and were poised to walk off. My heart sank, and Steve Harding went pale.

Just then, Leonardo DiCaprio came over and put his arm around Paul.

'I think Paul is right. If MGM had made this decision, it's their money and their choice. Let's support him,' he said.

Wow, what a wonderful young man, I thought. He was so young and yet so mature in his attitude: he realised, more than anyone else, that he actually stood to lose most if the film folded because his star (and asking price) was ascending, so the last thing he needed was any bad press.

By the end of our first week, Paul and a brilliant American production accountant re-worked the budget and schedule to something more sensible.

Having then submitted his new production plan to MGM, Paul received a call from Frank Mancuso, the (then) head of the studio, who seemed rather pissed off as he asked Paul to supply his full resume credits and to qualify why on earth he'd sent through an increased budget for approval. In fact, he seemed so incensed that he said he was flying in to meet Paul the following Monday with the express purpose of reducing the budget.

I remember we were filming on location in the grounds of a French château, Le Vicomte, quite a way from the main house which required golf buggies to get around as it was so large, and when word reached us that Mr Mancuso had arrived, Paul drove over to the house to greet him.

'Let's go to your office,' the studio chief suggested.

'I don't have one here, but we can go to the catering tent,' Paul said.

Mancuso looked Paul square in the eye and demanded to know, 'Who is responsible for this fiasco?'

'Your people, for hiring the wrong producer, and allowing an unrealistic budget to be signed off. But if you accept my budget, we'll finish the film,' Paul replied.

He also explained that Randall Wallace needed help as he relied heavily on both the 1st AD and his cameraman – who wasn't always terribly patient – and so adding extra pressure to him to work quicker would, Paul concluded, be disastrous.

'I'm going back to the hotel. I'll meet you tomorrow,' Mancuso snapped.

At that next meeting, having thought it over, he asked Paul: 'Can you guarantee me that if I give you the extra money, you'll finish the film for not a dollar more?'

'I can't promise you that,' Paul replied truthfully, 'as we might have the worst weather or someone might go sick, but I give you my word I will do my best to bring it in on time.'

'Well, you're not having a penny more!' he grunted, and headed back to LA.

Unfortunately, Paul spoke too soon about the weather as temperatures hit a very humid 100 degrees Fahrenheit, making it very difficult, especially when combined with the added heat from the large lamps. After six weeks, the heatwave subsided and torrential rain ensued to the point we had to lay down tracks over the sodden ground to be able to move people and equipment without sinking, and as we left the unit base each morning and drove to the location we waited, waited, and waited for a break in the rain, but on many days we just had to take cover in tents and cars.

Leonardo DiCaprio became bored and frustrated and would fool around a little, which I think tested Paul's patience, so I intervened: 'Paul, he's a young man just having a bit of fun and letting off steam to relieve the boredom, go easy on him,' I reasoned.

Mercifully, we managed to complete the film – if totally exhausted by the end.

The costumes, the sets and the locations were incredible, and by the end of shooting the crew were all behind Paul. And the catering – wow! On our first day, I remember sitting down in the tent and being served a wonderful Michelin-star standard lunch, with a carafe of water… and a bottle of wine each from Gerard Depardieu's vineyard. Paul was a little taken aback to be served wine at lunchtime on a working set, but I suggested it was a one-off gesture just to welcome him into the fold and so we could all raise a glass together. Silly me! It wasn't a one-off at all; it was a daily routine, as French crews don't see wine as alcohol, but as a necessary accompaniment to a meal. I don't think I've ever eaten so well on a set in my life, before or since.

I enjoyed my rare days off visiting galleries, parks and museums. I had hoped my son Martin might be able to travel across from London to spend some weekends with me, but he was actually becoming a much sought after assistant director in his own right and was busier than me, jetting all over the world. Long may it last.

After wrapping on the shoot, I was asked to travel back and forth to Paris for post-production for a few months, to be Paul's eyes and ears, which suited me wonderfully well as that had always been my favourite part of the whole process – the editing, the sound design, the effects, the music – that magical time when everything comes together and was such a joyous process to be involved with, in a fairly relaxed manner without the pressure of having actors sitting around and the clock ticking tens of thousands of dollars every second.

Anne Parillaud and Judith Godrèche were two of the French leading ladies in the film, and both were truly excellent. During a dubbing session one day in post-production, I asked former child star Judith what was next for her; she said she was heading to the USA to pursue a more international career. She did head to LA and, in fact, became a leading voice in the #MeToo movement, having encountered some of the worst Hollywood had to offer. Happily, she is now a successful film-maker and actress in her native France.

Once post-production was completed, everything was shipped back to LA and I remember a few months afterwards, Paul and I were in town and were invited to a preview of the movie. We flew back on a morning flight on August 31st, and just ahead of landing in London the Captain made a very solemn announcement over the PA system.

'I have just received news over my radio that Princess Diana has died in a car accident in Paris.'

There was total silence in the cabin – and total shock. I think everyone everywhere was dumbstruck that day.

We later learned the accident occurred in the Alma tunnel, which was on our daily commute during the shooting of the movie, and that sent a very cold shiver down both our spines.

Some months, or even a year, afterwards, Paul was sent a script about Princess Diana and although he agreed to read it, he wasn't so sure it was a subject he felt at ease dealing with – not least because it went into minute detail about the accident and concluded she had been assassinated. Paul passed it to me to read and asked for my thoughts – not that he'd base a decision on them, but he wanted my view.

As I read it, I experienced such an uncomfortable sensation that it caused me to say to Paul, 'Don't touch it.'

Paul nodded, and the script was duly returned.

Looking back on *The Man In The Iron Mask*, it's amazing to think that, yet again, the initial problems on the film all stemmed from incompetent people being hired and then agreeing to fit a script to a certain budget and schedule simply to suit the studio's whim, no matter how impractical to do so. But it kept Paul (and me) in work, so I mustn't complain too much.

Oh, the premiere in London was a Royal event too, with HRH Prince Charles as the guest of honour at the Odeon Leicester Square, with a party afterwards at The Banking Hall in which the design team set to work making everything look like it was from the period of Louis XIV. I was honoured to be invited and found it truly breathtaking.

Paul invited his grandson Ben to join him, who I think was around 15 then, as both his children had been to so many premieres and galas over the years, they felt he should spread such opportunities further around the family. At the pre-premiere reception, in an area where champagne was free-flowing, Paul said Ben could have just one glass. When Paul had to leave to join the line-up and be presented to the Royal party, he asked that I look after Ben. But the teenager kept disappearing to the bathroom, saying he was nervous. Fair enough. It wasn't until the film ended that we realised he had, in fact, been sneaking off to get more champagne as he was completely smashed!

Ben's ensuing hangover the next day obviously worried his mother, Susan, who took issue with Paul. But bless him, Ben said, 'No Mum, I ate some dodgy canapes.' A family drama was averted, and I think Ben was probably put off drinking fizz for quite a while afterwards!

CHAPTER 14

Castaway & Vertical Limit

Following *Iron Mask*, I discovered the industry had entered one of its slumps (again). The UK had a new government in 1997, and the Labour administration were extremely keen to support the arts, and in particular the film industry. But in the months-long build up to the election under Tory rule, and in the immediate aftermath when the party were formalising plans for new legislation and tax breaks, there was a period of uncertainty and a 'wait and see' attitude, so nothing much was being greenlit by the majors in the UK and Europe.

Again, I wondered how long it might be before my savings dwindled away on mortgage and bill payments. Fortunately, within a few months, Fred Gallo called. His wife was involved in setting up a new movie, *Castaway*, with director-writer Robert Zemeckis, which was set to star Tom Hanks as a FedEx troubleshooter who gets stranded on an uninhabited island when his plane crashes in the South Pacific.

The opening sequence was set in Moscow at the FedEx facility, and Fred said there was no way of doubling for – or faking it – they had to film in Russia. He said he had thought of me and asked if I'd help coordinate that element of the shoot.

FedEx provided access to their facilities as well as aeroplanes, trucks, uniforms, and logistical support. Their marketing department oversaw production through more than two years of filming in fact (between Moscow, Memphis and LA), and though the idea of a FedEx plane crashing must have given the company heart palpitations at first, the courier – which paid no money for product placement – saw a massive increase in brand awareness upon release.

If I could have only ever worked with one person in my whole career, then it would be Tom Hanks. He's so grounded, humble and polite. When it came to catering, I again recommended the Czech company we'd used on *The Saint*, and they worked out brilliantly, and on the first day one of the assistants went over to Tom Hanks to ask what he would like for lunch.

'I can get my own from the truck, thank you,' he replied. Sure enough, he proceeded to queue up for a meal and took it to eat with the crew – he sat with the carpenters and electricians chatting – and was so kind to everyone.

One of my tasks was to provide a car for Tom Hanks, and in asking which brand he would prefer, I suggested the latest Mercedes model was available – he said, 'No, no, I prefer a people carrier, please.'

I must have looked a little curious, as he then proceeded to explain that when he travelled to and from set, he liked to be with his make-up artist, the director of photography, and the costume designer so they could all chat about the day ahead, and the day they just had when on the way home.

There was no long list of riders either.

Oh, actually, there was one request.

Tom really wanted to visit Korolyov, which was the Russian Space City, Cosmonaut Town & Rocket Design Centre. It was their equivalent of NASA.

Just as you can imagine NASA receiving a request from a Russian actor to 'have a look around' would be met with a very firm 'no' – so it was that no Westerners were ever welcomed to Korolyov.

I said it was impossible and only the highest ranking military personnel with special permission were granted access.

'That's his only request,' the LA office told me, noting his starring in *Apollo 13* had really cemented his fascination in all things space, which was also highlighted more recently with the wonderful *Moonwalkers* exhibition in London, for which he provided the narration, telling the stories of the Apollo missions in intimate detail.

I wasn't about to upset the nicest man in showbusiness, but at the same time, I didn't quite know how I could pull off the impossible.

I called the facilities company, Three T, who were so brilliant on *The Saint*, to the point that they had even closed off Red Square for us, and spoke to its owner whose initial response was, 'That will never happen.' But when I explained it was for Tom Hanks and this was the one and only thing he wanted to do whilst in the city, he said, 'Well if we can get permission, Mr Hanks would only be allowed to go in alone. There can be no entourage or anyone else.'

I agreed, absolutely, and asked them to try.

The answer came back, 'No problem.'

Tom went along with just an interpreter, provided by the state of course, and when he returned, he was like a child who'd just been given free rein in a sweet shop. His eyes were wide, his grin was immovable and his enthusiasm was infectious.

He thanked me effusively, but I told him it was all due to Three T.

I think I was on the shoot for around three weeks and then the unit headed off, at which point – and happily – I discovered my son Martin had secured the position of First Assistant Director with the second unit, though not through me. He got the job having worked for Fred Gallo previously on *Angela's Ashes* in helping recce and photograph locations, which impressed the studio head, saying 'This is how it should be done.' It's always helpful to make a good impression.

Martin told me after a couple of months shooting, production paused so Tom could lose the 50 lbs he'd added during pre-production, whilst growing his hair and beard to look like he had been living on an island for four years. Then, after a further four-month break, they all returned to film his returning home scenes.

Overall, filming lasted for sixteen months!

***

Vertical Limit was a survival thriller movie which had shot on location in Pakistan, Queenstown, New Zealand and the United States. It was directed by Martin Campbell, not too long after his successful first James Bond adventure *Goldeneye*, and this new production starred Chris O'Donnell, Bill Paxton, Robin Tunney, and Scott Glenn.

At some point during the editing process, Martin realised there was a scene missing – don't ask me how or why, but obviously it created a big problem. There was no way the whole unit could ship out again to New Zealand (where adjacent scenes had been filmed) to pick up the shots, so it was decided to pull back to Pinewood for a few days of shooting.

I was quite happy to step in and assist Martin, who was an absolutely lovely man – a true 'darling' – with a very small crew to get the shots he needed.

After wrapping, Martin invited me, Paul, and some of the cast and crew to dinner at La Caprice, which was a very swanky restaurant just off Piccadilly, frequently visited by the fabulously rich and famous: Diana, Princess of Wales, and Princess Margaret were regular diners; Mick Jagger and Liz Taylor, too.

If only every job ended that way, rather than a P60 and worry about where the next pay cheque might come from.

It made me question, with the increasingly long gaps between bigger jobs, whether I should change career. It wasn't the first time such a thought had crossed my mind, and in desperation, I even considered working in hotels. I went for a meeting at one big place near Heathrow airport, dressed to impress, and the lady manager looked at me and said, 'You're overqualified.'

What she actually meant was that I was too old.

I even offered to do room cleaning – I wasn't proud – but still she shook her head. That's when I knew I needed to do something else within production if I was going to survive these long lulls: I didn't mean retraining as an accountant, legal expert or (heaven forbid) a typist, but rather use my existing expertise to find a niche which might involve not just one ad hoc production, but any number of films, even if shooting simultaneously.

I'd already experienced how certain brands were featured in films, such as the Volvo C70 on *The Saint*, FedEx on *Castaway* and so on, which created a bit of a buzz. This expanding world of 'product placement' also brought with it another revenue stream for producers – companies were willing to pay, sometimes huge amounts, to have their products featured alongside big stars.

It set me thinking…

CHAPTER 15

Mission Impossible II

Meanwhile, things picked up – as they have a habit of doing in this feast or famine business – as following the blockbuster success of the first *Mission*, Paramount Pictures and its star wanted a follow-up, a sequel. Indeed, the second instalment began cranking up in 1998 at Paramount's offices, where Paul and I were invited to meet the absolutely charming and wonderful John Woo, who had signed-on to direct. He was an interesting choice on Tom's part as he'd primarily been known for martial arts movies, though has since proven himself adept at pretty much every subject he's tackled.

Though, when I say Paramount 'offices', what I actually mean to say is 'portacabins' because the studio's lot was so incredibly busy with a swell of TV production that there wasn't room for much else. Though I loved Los Angeles ever since I very first visited – the climate is lovely, the buzz is wonderful and of course everyone is hustling or trying to get work in movies – so it was no great hardship! Plus, one of the nice things about being in prep is that you usually always get the weekend off, and I certainly made the most of my Saturdays and Sundays, immersing myself into LA life and culture.

During the week, we always lunched with John Woo and the office staff which usually meant Chinese food, though John Woo always insisted on paying – and out of his own pocket too – which I'd never experienced on a picture before or since.

We agreed to prep as much of the movie as possible in LA before moving out to Australia, where the bulk of the story and our production was set, with some final location work scheduled in Spain. Knowing we would be going to Sydney at the outset – as Tom was then married to Nicole Kidman and wanted to spend more time in her home country, which he loved – we just packed summer clothes, little knowing what was envisioned to be a six-month trip would turn into two years away!

You see, we could prep as much as we wanted but the one thing we did not have, which was quite crucial to the production starting, was a script.

William Goldman was the first writer to sign up but ultimately admitted that he could not come up with a good villain; that's when Robert Towne took over. John Woo had already planned several action sequences and Towne was primarily tasked with linking them, whilst Ronald D. Moore and Brannon Braga took a pass at the script. All the time this was going on, Paul was being shown outline stories, which it transpired Tom Cruise wasn't actually very keen on, but it at least gave Paul an idea of the scale and ambition of the film, and he was able to start hiring some key crew in Australia. After seven months, and countless Chinese lunches, we were still waiting for an approved script to be delivered…

It was then that Tom's producer partner, Paula Wagner, announced they wanted Andrew Lesnie as our Director of Photography – but we had already filmed some camera tests with Thandie [now Thandiwe] Newton and the cameraman hired for those tests had been given a six-week guarantee by the studio. However, Paula said that when Tom viewed the tests, he decided that although Thandie was perfect, the cinematographer was not and should be replaced. The dismissed cameraman was on a $25,000-a-week contract and was therefore paid off for those six guaranteed weeks with $150,000 for doing just one day's work.

Paula Wagner, it would be fair to say, didn't have an in-depth knowledge about the technicalities of making a film, so when Andrew Lesnie looked up at John Woo during their first meeting and asked, 'What sort of film stock will you be using on the movie?' and John didn't quite understand the question – as he'd been used to his cameraman turning up and rolling cameras with the type of stock never being mentioned, as long as it was high speed – Paula Wagner decided to pipe up with, 'Well, we want to make this film in colour.'

Andrew looked across the table at Paul and raised his eyebrows.

Next, the key crew headed off on a recce across Spain – from Barcelona down to Malaga – looking for locations for sequences in the film that we still didn't have a script for. We did know that the storyline was to see IMF Agent Ethan Hunt (Tom Cruise) sent on a mission to retrieve and destroy the supply of a genetically created disease called Chimera. Along the way, we knew he'd be competing with a terrorist gang whilst recruiting a professional thief and ex-girlfriend of an IMF rogue agent to trace the agent to Sydney. Or something like that.

Spain, it had been decided by Tom, was where the chemicals in the story were being developed. Paul engaged a local production manager to set up a unit in Granada and await further information.

It was then that studio heads Sherry Lansing and Fred Gallo decreed they were not going to green-light the film unless $10million was cut from the proposed budget, and were adamant the film had to come in under $100million. Though the irony was that we didn't have a final script, nor a final schedule, nor budget either. It was 'best guess' time based on $300,000 per day spend.

Nevertheless, Paul was asked to inform Tom that if we did not shave a tenth off our costs, then the film would not go ahead. Rather than tear pages out of the script, Paul suggested that if they did not go to Spain – and instead, found locations to double in Australia – it would save time and, in discussion with the production accountant and designer, he calculated that it would, in fact, cut around $9million. Tom was resistant at first, but when he realised the studio heads were not going to budge on their decision, he relented. First and foremost, Tom is a canny businessman.

***

With the script being 'a couple of weeks away from completion' I flew to Sydney with Paul, arriving at 6am one Saturday morning, where our local production manager insisted she wanted to meet us in arrivals and arrange our onward journey to the hotel. I said she should not worry at such an early hour, and we would see her later at the production meeting, for which she would surely have more important things to prepare. But no, she was quite adamant that she wanted to be at the airport to meet us.

That was appreciated actually, as I knew we would be very tired. Having someone to assist, take the pressure off carrying bags and find the production cars would be a help.

I guess we had 8 or 9 suitcases – as we anticipated being there for quite a few months – including clothes, laptops, paperwork, and the like. Though there were no trolleys to be found in Sydney airport nor any porters, so I ran around the luggage hall looking for a way to try and gather everything, but to no avail. I had a eureka moment and phoned our awaiting production manager to explain we were stuck by the belt with lots of heavy bags, as I felt sure she would have a solution or at least be able to speak to someone landside. I had been a production manager myself and had always foreseen situations like this.

'Oh, I can't help you,' she whined without even attempting to summon some assistance from one of the many desks near where she was waiting. We were not terribly impressed, and that should have in fact warned us of what was to come.

Paul and I slid bags across the cavernous arrivals area, and in a sort of tag-race between us, piled up the luggage by the exit door before Paul opened it and started pushing the bags out towards our beaming production manager. She stood motionless, watching, never offering to help, and it clearly never occurred to her we had just flown 14 hours and were exhausted, with all sorts lined up to do later in the day.

'You know what,' I said to her quietly as she bounded over to us with a wide smile once all the bags had been pushed through, 'if this is the beginning, you may as well pack *your* bags!'

'What did you say?' Paul asked.

I smiled warmly – ever the diplomat.

Within a few weeks, the production manager proved to be out of her depth and was 'let go'. Fortunately, we received a recommendation about a lady named Anne Bruning who had served as PM on a dozen or so Australian films, and whilst none of them had been huge blockbusters, we were assured that she was extremely capable and diligent. She turned out to be an absolute darling, as were her crew. She brought with her three young female assistants who were not only extremely efficient and brilliant at their work, but they could also have easily been models – they were beautiful, and always so very well dressed. It was hugely amusing to note how there was a steady stream of male crew members coming by the office each day with odd little errands, queries, and almost pointless questions when our trio were in. There wasn't anything inappropriate I should add, but I dare say the chaps were maybe hopeful of being invited on a date – they never were!

The whole pre-production process had been hampered by the lack of a script, so when pages did filter through to us, we were elated, until we realised they were a few at a time and even then some were redacted with various parts blanked out to preserve secrecy. Nevertheless, we were expected to schedule, budget and storyboard them. Of course, script delays also meant actors who had been cast in the various roles couldn't be given exact start dates, just rough blocks, which meant they were all paid and received overtime regardless of whether they were going to begin shooting; I'm sure they were happy to be drawing fees without having to work, but it was all adding to the budget! There were some pretty big names involved too: Anthony Hopkins, Ving Rhames, Brendan Gleeson, Dougray Scott, and the aforementioned Thandie to name but a few.

We had arrived in Australia December 1998 and started filming in the following April, but just ahead of rolling cameras the biggest hailstorm in Australian history – a supercell – hit. It developed south of Sydney on the afternoon of Wednesday, 14 April 1999, and struck the city's eastern suburbs, including the central business district, later that evening. It proved to be the costliest natural disaster in Australian insurance history, causing extensive damage along the east coast of New South Wales, dropping an estimated 500,000 tonnes of hailstones – many being the size of tennis balls – which damaged not only the stage roofs, but also the fleet of 31 cars which I'd arranged for our use in a product placement deal with Avis. There were all write-offs.

After everything had been cleared, repaired, and replaced, we finally started filming. But Paul raised a serious concern after the first days rushes arrived: there was a scene at a racecourse where Dougray Scott (playing Ambrose, the rogue IMF agent) is looking through a window. We couldn't help but see that the window was absolutely covered in dirty and greasy fingerprints, but the cameraman clearly hadn't noticed. Paul asked Tom if he had seen anything untoward (as he'd watched it on a monitor in his trailer), but when he said he hadn't, Paul suggested Tom should go to the viewing theatre and run it on the large screen. When he emerged a few minutes later, Tom was furious.

It was a sloppy error that should never had got past Andrew Lesnie, but as he appeared to be more and more dishevelled each day in the build up to us rolling cameras, there had already been a genuine concern that he was not going to last the course.

Tom thought for a moment before saying, 'You're the producer Paul, you need to fire him!'

In the event, Andrew Lesnie resigned over what Paramount called 'stylistic differences'.

In truth, he was fired but was allowed to say he resigned in order to save face.

Lesnie was not the first key creative to leave, as original production designer, Owen Paterson, had already gone (by 'mutual agreement') and Tom Saunders was brought in as his replacement. Some crew voiced their unease at all these changes and suggested it should instead be called 'the impossible mission.'

Of course, Paramount put a positive spin on things in reporting Lesnie's departure as being 'very amicable' and assured everyone that the change would not cause any delays. The same studio spokesperson was quoted in trade journals as saying, 'The budget is nowhere near triple digits and closer to $80 million.'

Oh, yes?

Jeffrey Kimball was appointed as our new director of photography; he was a big character who had collaborated with Tom on *Top Gun* and quickly became a great asset to the production. Though, when Jeffrey asked if he could bring along his regular focus-puller from America, who he was used to collaborating with and particularly because he realised there would be so much high-speed action that he'd need someone able to work quickly, that gave us major headaches with the Australian trade bodies.

The film industry was very unionised at that time in Australia, causing Paul to remark it was like 'working in England in the 1960s'. In fact, at our first big unit meeting in Sydney, the opening line from the shop steward was, 'We've heard about you Americans and your way of working, and we will not be working overtime. We have 24 hours in our day and it is comprised of 8 hours work, 8 hours relaxation and entertaining, and 8 hours sleep and that will not be changing.'

What a welcome!

Of course, some discussions and trade-offs were reached to ensure everyone was happy – eventually.

Oh, I should add we had a wonderful Australian costume designer named Lizzy Gardiner, who had won an Oscar for her work on *The Adventures of Priscilla, Queen of the Desert*. Lizzy asked Tom early on about how he visualised the 'look' of his character, Ethan Hunt. He suggested 'a sort of smart-casual'.

'You'll stand out like a pair of dog's bollocks in the desert,' Lizzy said, whilst realising she was putting her foot well and truly in it by the reaction on Tom's face.

There was a deathly silence and we all thought, 'That's the end of Lizzy.'

After a pause, which seemed like several minutes, Tom pondered, 'So what do you think I should look like?'

'The sort of outfits Steve McQueen wore: all designer clothes, but ones that look lived in. They give a certain edge and style,' Lizzy replied.

Tom immediately warmed to her suggestion; well, who would not want to be compared to Steve McQueen?

'I think that's a very good idea, but we'll have to get wardrobe to wear them down,' he added.

It meant none of the clothes could be returned, once worn in, so if they did not fit perfectly or if Tom did not like them, we would still have to pay. Consequently, at the end of production we had a massive 'wardrobe sale' with crew members buying designer jackets, sweaters, and shirts for just $5 apiece.

Paula Wagner asked, 'Is every job filled now?' as she looked down the crew list.

'Yes, I believe so,' Paul replied.

'Hang on,' she queried, 'who is this person here you've got down as Tom's stand in?'

'He's an Australian guy. He is five foot six tall and that is what he does for a living.'

'Well, he won't be acceptable to Tom,' Paula replied dryly, 'as he wants the same person we used on *Eyes Wide Shut* – because he was wonderful.'

A stand-in does just that – they stand on set when the camera team are lighting a shot, to save the artist having to hang around unnecessarily. It is not a particularly demanding or skilled job, and Paul reasoned, 'Flying someone in from London to stay here for the whole shoot will be very expensive.'

'Well, you'll have to make it work!' she replied.

'Who was he Paula? What was his name?'

'I've no idea… but he was very good.' was her parting comment.

As luck would have it, our production accountant had also been on *Eyes Wide Shut*, so Paul popped across to ask, 'Who was Tom's stand in?'

'Tom never had a stand-in,' he replied, 'we just used the clapper loader.'

Stanley Kubrick certainly would not have wanted to pay a stand-in so that made sense, but you can understand why sometimes Paul said he felt 102 years old!

***

My personal relationship with Paul intensified during *Mission: Impossible II*. We were away for almost two years, and on every location up until then, I had made a point of booking Paul and I separate rooms in hotels. Although no one spoke about it, our being together seemed common knowledge, so I thought, as we were going to have apartments in Sydney, we might as well just share one. No one flinched.

Fred Gallo announced he was flying over for a set visit soon after we'd started, and to do that thing studio heads like to do – putting his arm around everyone and say how wonderful things are. Which is always worrying.

John Woo suggested he wanted to host a dinner in Fred's honour (and didn't suggest a Chinese restaurant for a change). It was all a little last minute, with sixteen people attending, and consequently we were all a little crammed into a popular venue who were very keen to accommodate us. I found myself totally hemmed in and halfway through the meal made a couple of polite, 'Could you excuse me?' comments as I needed to visit the bathroom, which fell on deaf ears, I finally erupted with 'For God's sake I need to get out!'

Without missing a beat, John Woo looked at me and said, 'How do you think I feel?'

He was not referring to needing the bathroom but rather the enormity of the project. We couldn't help but laugh.

Fred Gallo felt satisfied after meeting us that all was running smoothly and returned to LA to tell everyone he had been over and 'fixed it all' – not that there was anything to fix. That's the bullshit of Hollywood.

Everything was indeed running smoothly until about two or three weeks in, when Tom Cruise asked Paul a quite bizarre and unnerving question.

'How long has Dougray Scott been shooting with us?'

Paul said he had been on set for about 12 days at that point.

'How much would it cost to reshoot those days?' Tom asked.

Paul thought for a moment, realising it may well be a 'damned if I do and damned if I don't' moment as Tom clearly seemed unhappy about something.

'Four to five million,' Paul replied – hoping it was enough of a deterrent to put thoughts of replacing the actor out of Tom's mind.

It obviously was, and despite never saying anything to us about what was bugging him, Tom took Dougray to one side and in a very animated conversation, obviously read him the riot act about something. All was resolved, and we moved on – with nothing ever being mentioned again.

Though one major problem arose a little while later when Dougray suffered an accident during the filming of the motorbike chase sequence and damaged his shoulder quite badly. The insurers asked us to produce variances on what we could continue shooting, but next on the schedule was a car chase sequence with him, and it was very apparent that we would not be able to film it with Dougray, so schedules had to be altered and the sequence was pushed back.

This was all after being in Sydney for a year by the way, and a consequence of our overrun was that Dougray couldn't complete his part in time to play Wolverine in *The X Men* movie – it went to Hugh Jackman instead.

After moving back to LA, we built a large descender rig in one of the hangars at the airport, as we needed to film Tom jumping out of a building at great height in a carefully controlled environment. Tom has never shied away from stunts, and in fact the more daring the better as far as he was concerned: he took on all the rock-climbing scenes at the opening of the movie, which were filmed in Utah, hundreds, and thousands of feet off the ground. John Woo loved the sense of danger too!

After spending six further months in LA on this and other sequences (including some of the scenes previously set to shoot in Spain), we had to nip back to Sydney for a month to shoot the postponed climax to the motorbike chase with Dougray, from where we returned to LA once more to wrap everything. From beginning to end, I spent two years of my life on the movie and the only time I got to go home was for Christmas 1999 – and even that was a flying visit. Though I was quite fortunate in being able to ship back a case of an exciting New Zealand wine which had proven so popular in the UK that it was terribly difficult (and expensive) to get hold of, Cloudy Bay. It was plentiful in my house over that holiday!

I had asked my son Martin if he would move into my home during my absence, to look after my two cats. The idea pleased Martin greatly as it meant he could give up his rented accommodation and did not have to pay any costs for two whole years. Though my one stipulation was that my bedroom door was to remain closed and the cats should not be allowed in there, and of course Martin readily agreed. Three weeks later, he sent me a photograph of both cats lying across my bed having the most wonderful chilled out time with the caption, 'Wish you were here?'

Ten weeks after wrapping, John Woo delivered the first cut of the film to the Paramount screening room. We all filed in with great enthusiasm and excitement but three long hours later when the lights went up, the feeling had changed dramatically. Quite honestly, Paul said it was the most boring movie he had ever sat through and his fellow audience members (the studio senior executives) did not quite know what to say either. John had shot so much footage, on so many cameras, that there was quite simply just too much of everything – it lacked focus, cohesion, and a clear narrative. In short, it was an overlong mess.

The key creative talent were all called in to the executives' offices, and on the way over Paula Wagner said to Paul, 'We are all in a state of shock.' Paul told me he bumped into John Goldwyn, who was then Head of Production, in the men's room, who declared, 'This is un-releasable.'

With those words still ringing in his ears, Paul was even more shocked when the studio executives all looked at him, questionably. They were waiting for Paul's solution.

Realising he was on the spot, Paul summarised the situation: 'OK. We have dubbing dates booked, music recording sessions booked and it is not as though we just have to take ten minutes out, we have to cut at least an hour and still come up with a releasable film.'

Paula Wagner asked, 'Have you got any ideas?'

Paul suggested everyone should sleep on it, and the next morning, Paula Wagner, seemingly devoid of suggestions herself, asked Paul if he had had any thoughts overnight.

'We need Stuart Baird,' Paul suggested.

Stuart was not only an old friend of Paul's, but he is also one of the finest film editors in the business and has a first-class reputation for being able to 'fix' a film.

'I'll mention it to Tom,' Paula replied.

The next day, a Saturday, she called Paul saying Tom was worried about the effect it might have on John Woo's reputation.

'Paula, we have *got* to bring this to a head. I consider John a friend and my business partner, but we have a problem here,' Paul replied.

Paula asked to meet Stuart.

'I don't even know if he is available,' he told her, 'I haven't asked because there is no point unless you are all serious.'

Paula said she wanted to bike a script to Stuart's house and asked if he would then meet Tom in the editing room on Monday morning. John Woo, meanwhile, had not even been brought into the conversation and knew nothing about it.

Paul phoned Stuart and asked what he was up to.

'Just taking it easy today – how about dinner tomorrow?' Stuart asked.

'I need to have lunch with you,' Paul said earnestly.

'Paul, I can't…'

'Stuart, it will be very beneficial to you, and if you are my pal, you'll meet me,' Paul pleaded.

Stuart told Paul he was already committed to a lunch in Malibu and could not change it, but suggested Paul and I could meet him there. On arriving at the restaurant, we found Stuart deep in conversation with Mel Gibson.

'Why don't you join us?' Mel asked.

'No! We can't!' Paul replied, much to Stuart's surprise, 'I need Stuart to myself.'

'What's all this about Paul?' Stuart asked curtly.

Paul took Stuart aside and told him about the project and the problem with which we were now faced. He gave Stuart the script and asked to meet at the studio first thing on Monday morning to run the film and then meet with Tom afterwards.

'Your agent will get you a good deal, as we're desperate people!' Paul concluded.

On the Monday morning, Stuart arrived at Paramount, having read the script, grimaced a bit and disappeared into the viewing theatre to watch the 3-hour cut.

Afterwards, he turned to Paul and said, 'This is a massive job, there is so much footage.'

He paused.

'OK. I will do it, providing I have carte blanche.'

'I can't promise that, Stuart, Tom is producing as well as starring – you'd have to clear it with him.'

'OK, that's fine,' Stuart said. 'Can I meet him at 10am tomorrow?'

It was agreed, and the next day Stuart arrived early, and Tom… well, Tom arrived an hour late at 11am and held his hand out to greet Stuart.

Stuart looked at his watch, and then proceeded to sit with Tom to run the film, along the way making suggestions about how he'd recut, and each time Tom said 'Oh no, you can't cut that part because…'

After three or four such interjections, Stuart raised an eyebrow and asked, 'I thought you wanted me to come up with an edit which, if any good, we can move on from?'

Tom thought about it for a moment and replied, 'Come up with a cut and we'll take it from there.'

Stuart did exactly that, though along the way he had a couple of minor differences of opinion with Tom – after all, they are both extraordinarily strong characters – but ultimately Tom knew that Stuart had done a brilliant job, and more importantly would make a lot of money for the producers and the studio.

On a $125million budget (it did exceed $100million despite earlier warnings from the studio chiefs) the film grossed nearly $550million. Stuart did not receive a credit, but then again, he rarely did on the films he was parachuted in to save, though he did console himself with a very handsome fee.

***

On *M:i2*, as the marketing people liked to dub it, I also got more and more involved in product placement – after all, what company would not want to be associated with the 'next Tom Cruise movie'? (Luckily, they didn't see that first cut, or they might have thought otherwise!).

There was a specialist company in LA, also with offices in Europe, called Propaganda, which oversaw product placement. That is to say, getting brands visibly involved in movies. They oversaw pretty much everything on *M:i2*, and I was their point of liaison. Companies such as Avis, Audi, Nokia phones,

Triumph motorcycles, Oakley sunglasses, Bulgari jewellery, Kodak cameras and so many more were literally queuing up to offer products – and cash for them being in shot. It is free money for producers, and if the hero uses the products it usually attracts a premium.

One extra side-benefit is the 'freebies'. I asked for three Audi's – one for Tom, one for the US producer and one for John Woo to use during production. At the end of filming, Tom said, 'I'd like to keep this car and have another when I get back to Los Angeles.'

I said, 'Hmmm. I will see what I can do.'

Audi readily agreed, as the thought of Tom Cruise being pictured out-and-about in an A8 model was publicity of which they could only ever dream. Well, let me tell you that in Hollywood, dreams do come true – at the right price.

Tom then said the same about the Triumph motorbike, and how he would like one back home. He got that one too.

I guess being the star has its benefits!

Eventually, it came to the premiere at Mann's Chinese Theatre in Los Angeles on May 18th, 2000, which was a big glitzy affair followed by a party in Westwood Village, in a car park. A car park! But boy, did the production designers transform that parking lot into something extraordinary, almost akin to a set from the movie itself – it was a night I will never forget.

We all said our goodbyes, and I returned to London.

***

Roll on to 2005 and StudioCanal announced they were going to remake Jean-Pierre Melville's classic 1970 film noir *Le Cercle Rouge (1970)* in the English language, entitled *The Red Circle* with John Woo attached to direct – and he wanted Paul to produce. It seemed more of a full circle for me, in terms of my career, as my new bosses, StudioCanal, had earlier bought the Weintraub Film Library where I had started work at Pinewood Studios!

The original 1970 French film starred Alain Delon as a thief released from prison the same day a murderer escapes police custody and they pair up to commit a daring heist. With lots of action, car chases and fighting, I could see why John Woo was signed for it.

Unfortunately, there was just one problem – the same one – there wasn't a finished script.

I remember Paul saying, 'Here we go again.'

Paul and I met with John in London where he explained some really wonderful ideas, including a scene where the two outlaws are being chased through a quaint English village.

'It would be good if the car goes through the pub, and through a conservatory like this…' as John demonstrated it all with a model and toy cars, showing us exactly how he would do it and where the cameras should be placed. Talk about boys in a toy shop!

M:i2 had been a big-budget studio production with Tom Cruise, whereas this project was a modest production in comparison, and without Tom Cruise. However, Paul started looking at potential locations and costing up some of the sequences.

Upon submitting an initial budget to StudioCanal, they immediately jumped on Paul's back, lecturing him about economics and how Working Title (who they had financed some films with in the UK) would 'never spend this sort of money on this type of film'. Paul's blood pressure was obviously heading upwards as he snapped, 'Working Title wouldn't hire John Woo! He is going to make you an exceptionally good commercial movie here.'

But they continued to beat Paul up over every single entry in the budget he had prepared and demanded whole scenes be cut – and this was despite still not having a full script – to the point that it seemed that most of the action had been replaced with (cheaper) dialogue-heavy dramatic scenes. John Woo is very much an action director, so it seemed completely bizarre that they should be trying to turn the film into one devoid of any, and I know too well how during *M:i2* John quickly got bored with Tom and Thandie in their dialogue scenes, and kept suggesting they do all their talking on motorbikes whilst jumping over buildings, so it was obvious to me that there was very much a clash of creatives here.

Despite having a full art department, accounts, production, and locations managers hard at work, the whole project was cancelled when StudioCanal realised their aspirations vastly exceeded their pockets. We all felt so sorry for John Woo.

When the company ordered the picture to close down, Paul explained that they had to first put the crew on notice (usually two weeks), but the French paymasters argued that everyone should be fired there and then and not receive a penny more.

We wasted the best part of six months of our lives and had a thoroughly unhappy, miserable time on the project – as did John. The remake never came to anything, and John moved on to other projects though does from time-to-time suggest he would like another chance at remaking it.

Who knows …

CHAPTER 16

Providing Product Placement

After two long years on *M:i2* and the abandoned *Red Circle* episode, Paul was thinking about packing it all in. He'd already retired once, but now he was approaching 70 and felt he'd had enough, not so much of filmmaking but the politics and personalities which had all changed massively in more recent years. I could understand, but I wanted to carry on working because I loved it – I loved being around film sets and film studios. Having dipped my toe into the world of product placement, and having worked so well with Propaganda, I decided that perhaps it was an area of the business I should pursue full-time.

With production costs soaring, producers were looking at all sorts of ways to bring costs down, be it with government incentives, tax breaks and any other 'soft money' – and product placement was a key contributor to the budget's bottom line as it was free money in exchange for featuring merchandise and products. 'Propaganda' was at the forefront of the business but didn't have a London office. So, I suggested the idea, flew to Geneva to meet with the partners and they offered me the role which I started in 2001.

Film business in the UK was buoyant. Though admittedly, with a looming threat of a SAG actor's strike that year, coupled with the outbreak of the foot-and-mouth livestock virus which shut off many countryside locations, and a general nervousness by many foreign filmmakers and actors about travelling post-September 11, things had quietened a little. Whilst the UK offered a favourable dollar to pound exchange rate, and attractive tax breaks, the lure of 'free' funds coming in on top proved extra tempting to the *Bond* and *Tomb Raider* producers to remain in the UK... and I was certainly willing to tempt them and others as best I could.

Propaganda had excellent links with major and high-end companies in technology, jewellery, cars, motorbikes, alcohol, foodstuffs, transport, and aviation – you name it, they knew someone.

On approaching productions, I could obviously show the great track record Propaganda had, and then I would offer to read their script and proceed to break it down and identify potential opportunities and partners.

For example, one of my first projects was with acclaimed French director Claude Lelouch who was making a film entitled *And Now... Ladies and Gentlemen*, about a female French jazz singer (Patricia Kaas) and a British jewel thief (Jeremy Irons) who likes to target extremely expensive jewellers. They fall in love and embark upon a tour of the world in a gorgeous sailing boat named 'Ladies and Gentlemen', though he cannot quite give up his old ways of making a living.

It is a very stylised film, beautifully lit with wonderfully exotic locations in the vein of glossy widescreen 1960s romantic comedies centring on glamorous people in faraway places and was co-produced by an old Warner Bros. friend, Rick Senat, who had been the studio's Business Affairs Executive for 27 years. Rick had retired to become a freelancer and co-producer of this film with his old friend Lelouch. Rick also asked Paul Hitchcock to postpone his retirement plans to join him, and they, in turn, engaged me to see how I could help with the budget, which, as with all independently financed films, was tight.

When I read the script, I immediately said, 'This is perfect for Bulgari.' I had collaborated with the company on *M:i2*, so I had an idea of the type of thing they'd find appealing, and being the prized booty of an international jewel thief is actually quite an enviable honour!

Companies like Bulgari have huge marketing budgets and just as they will pay for billboards and TV ads, they will pay handsomely to be featured in a film that they feel targets their perfect audience. Propaganda offered their services to producers without a fee or commission – instead, they charged the supplier, so producers were in a win-win situation.

However, when my Bulgari idea was discussed with Lelouch, he point-blankly refused, reasoning that he had a long-standing association with Chopard, and was adamant that Chopard would be featured. Whilst Chopard were indeed happy to offer their services and products, they were not prepared to pay on top; they felt they were already doing the film a service.

I returned to my boss, Rueben, at Propaganda and said Lelouch was not for budging.

'OK, let's all meet in Paris. Can you get Lelouch there and we'll make him an offer he cannot refuse?' Rueben asked. I said sure, and he arranged to fly in from Rome with a Bulgari representative. Lelouch attended with his wife and a Canal+ executive (they were financing the film), but his grumpy demeanour made it evident he was not interested.

'Chopard will do the film,' he affirmed.

The Bulgari rep said, 'How about we supply the jewellery for the film, and your lovely wife can choose any necklace she would like, whilst you can choose any one of our watches. Are Chopard offering that too?'

Bulgari watches range from a few thousand to tens of thousands of pounds, I should mention, and necklaces – well, they were equally if not more expensive.

Lelouch's expression turned from a frown to a quizzical one as he looked across the table to his wife, who nodded affirmatively.

'Maybe Bulgari would be an interesting choice after all…' he graciously suggested!

The jewellers also assisted in allowing us to use their stores and real gems in every one of our scenes in London and Fez, Morocco. Each day, caseloads duly arrived in armoured vans, with Bulgari's armed security standing guard before shooting began, at the end of each day, and everything was packed away and transported back to base in the same armoured vans. It never cost the production a penny, let alone any headaches for the props department in having to replicate such fine pieces.

Lelouch was a big name in French cinema, and once the film had been completed we heard that the Cannes Film Festival wanted to screen it on the closing night of the 2002 festival. It was a huge honour and a great PR opportunity – for which of course Bulgari happily stepped in to dress the red-carpet arrivals in their jewellery for the world's press to photograph.

***

In 2003, I had been with Propaganda for over two years and worked on over 20 films, but thought that it was time to set out on my own, as having made so many contacts (many of whom I brought to the table myself I should add) it seemed the opportune moment to be master of my own destiny again.

The first and one of the most exciting, and in many ways challenging, productions I had ever worked on was the feature film version of *Phantom of the Opera*. I say challenging primarily because it is a story set in the 1880s, and thinking of modern-day companies who would therefore be interested or even be relevant to product placement is a bit of a head scratcher. Fortunately, I knew the theatre show and how the finale involves a huge chandelier, so my thoughts immediately turned to Swarovski crystals. I've always maintained that 'you just need a bit of imagination' when you read a script, so I made a call to Nadja Swarovski to tell her I had the perfect vehicle for her – not only for the chandelier, but jewellery, and costumes, of which many were adorned with crystals.

Paul was one of the producers and had actually been attached to the project since the late 1980s when Warner Bros. were involved, but at the time, Andrew Lloyd-Webber was going through a divorce, and the director Joel Schumacher had become very much in demand after helming two *Batman* movies, and *Phantom* was shelved. However, in early 2003, Paul received a call from Andrew Lloyd-Webber's office saying they had bought the rights back from Warner's and were making the film as an independent UK production, which the impresario was personally financing and wondered if Paul would Exec Produce.

The budget was generous by British independent standards, though extremely tight for the scope and scale of this film, as the sets alone cost £13million!

Joel Schumacher was demanding, creatively, but wanted to employ the very best cameraman, production designer, line producer, costume designer and all the key creative personnel – he hadn't made a film in the UK before, so didn't arrive with any crew in tow, unlike many other directors who often fall in love with a certain cameraman, or designer and want to use them on every single film they make – regardless of whether they are the right person for that film or not.

Paul, in fact, said that in all his years in the business, this film undoubtedly had the most perfect crew – everyone from hairdressers, prosthetics, carpenters, electricians, runners… you name it. You could not fault a single aspect.

Tony Pratt was the brilliant production designer, but sadly did not get the accolades he deserved for the simple reason everyone thought they filmed in the Paris Opera House and not a recreation of it on stage E in Pinewood Studios – the sets were so fantastic that no one believed they were not real!

On the Pinewood backlot there were exterior sets constructed of the theatre and some Parisian shops adjacent – one of which was a Swarovski Jewellery frontage. It was, after all, a fictional film, so it did not really matter that the company was not around before 1880.

The wonderful chandelier in the opera house cost $1million, plus we had two others which, although not as pricey, were still very valuable – a metal one which was the one that 'dropped', plus a smaller model for certain effects scenes. The company sent a team from Austria to build and maintain the pieces, as they did not want anyone else to touch them. It saved the production $1million thanks to the 'product placement' of that centrepiece alone, so it was hugely significant and helpful, particularly as Joel was always saying to Paul, 'We need more money – ask Andrew to sell another one of his Pre-Raphaelite paintings!'

Andrew was very much hands-on, and in fact, Paul had given up his large office at Pinewood – as it was one of the few en-suite executives rooms then – and Andrew brought in a little piano where he composed some of the additional music for the movie that wasn't in the stage show. The final piece, Love Never Dies, he composed in just a couple of weeks.

It was a fantastic experience and a film I was immensely proud of being involved with, as was Swarovski, which received a lot of screen time and plaudits. The film cost $70million in the end, and although it only went on to gross $154.6 million and therefore was not regarded as an immediate runaway success by Hollywood standards, it was widely praised for its visuals and acting.

Production designer Peter Lamont, an old friend, had seen the chandelier Swarovski had designed for *Phantom*, and when it came to *Casino Royale (2006)*, for which he designed the sets, I discussed having Swarovski chandeliers as the heart of the casino with him. Director Martin Campbell, another old friend, thought it would be great and readily agreed, asking it to be 'as opulent as possible'. Swarovski were already supplying jewellery and, if you watch the film carefully, you will see their logo at the airport stores sequence. Peter discussed various options with them, finally choosing one that was opulence personified, though upon then taking that choice to Martin Campbell, Peter was told, 'It's not big enough'. There was no discussion, we were simply told a Czech company was being drafted-in instead, which put Swarovski's nose out and made my position a little awkward to say the least, given the support and investment the jeweller had given on the last Bond movie (*Die Another Day*) as well as this one. These things happen, of course.

Whilst admittedly I was left somewhat smarting by letting Swarovski down, I was also at a crossroads in my life. *Casino Royale* had shipped out of the UK – funnily enough, to my home city of Prague – partly because of its Eastern European setting, but primarily to take advantage of lower production costs plus appealing tax incentives when changes to the UK tax system and a weakened dollar meant the UK had become a comparatively expensive place to shoot in 2005. There was a worry that other big productions might follow 007 to the East, and it coincided with Paul saying in 2006 that he was definitely going to wind down. Whilst I could have continued working in the product placement arena, though perhaps having to relocate to the East myself and follow the work, I made the choice to retire. It was the right time, so Paul and I began the process of packing away our respective offices… when the phone rang.

CHAPTER 17

Fred Claus

Warner Bros. had been developing a Christmas comedy for a while and had, in fact, set up offices at Pinewood about six months prior. The story centred on Santa's brother, Fred, who had not quite lived up to his siblings' example and had been forced to move to the North Pole to help out with Christmas – it was very much a vehicle for Vince Vaughn, and on paper sounded amusing.

They called Paul and asked if he would help out.

He was in two minds about whether to take on the film, especially knowing I was closing my company down at his suggestion that we could spend more time together, so asked if I would consider being his Executive Assistant on the movie – for one last time. It was to be our movie swan song together, if you like.

No sooner had Paul signed than he realised he had unwittingly inherited a terrible mess. Same old, same old.

The producer (and writer) was Jessie Nelson, who had achieved critical success with her directorial debut *Corina Corina* (1994) – but she wasn't directing this. That honour went to David Dobkin who had worked, most notably, with Vince Vaughn on *Wedding Crashers* (2005).

The first and major problem Paul encountered was that six months in nobody had yet come to terms with how to shoot the movie or produce a concept of how it would all work. You see, it was to feature lots of little helper Elves, and when queried about this the Line Producer explained to Paul that 'most of them will have head replacements', meaning that well-known artists' heads would be superimposed whilst, it had been suggested by someone along the way, children could be used for the bodies. Paul declared the idea ludicrous as they are totally different types of characters to adults, plus they would have needed hours in make-up in preparation for the effects, and with strict working hour limits for children, it would mean they would have ended up having about 10 minutes a day on set. The Line Producer admitted she had no experience of CGI, and the Production Manager had only ever previously been a Production Co-ordinator and this was her first film in this new capacity – it did not instil confidence.

Paul insisted the Line Producer – who is very much the nuts-and-bolts person on the floor day to day – be replaced, which caused a lot of upset, leading to accusations of Paul being 'hard and horrible'. But after six months of being no further along, the studio agreed and backed him. (The lady in question went on to another film and was fired after just 3 weeks, and then a third soon afterwards, making it a hat-trick of disasters.)

In July 2006, the 007 Stage at Pinewood, which was to house Santa's North Pole workshop, caught fire and burned down during the dismantling of a set that had been used on *Casino Royale*. It threw our production into a bit of a panic as it was to house a huge, huge set that other stages at Pinewood were not big enough to hold.

After some frantic rescheduling and planning, we moved those few sequences out to Cardington, a former RAF base in Bedfordshire that had seen airship hangars converted into sound stages and had recently been used on *Batman Begins* (2005).

Meanwhile, Warner Bros. had set a release date – Christmas 2007. It was a Christmas movie after all, so could not really be released any other time. David Dobkin kept telling Paul about his contracted dates and Vince Vaughn's availability window, meaning we had to start shooting quite soon, or else.

Paul suggested that if we could find 'little people' that could be our way forward – but we would need a lot of them. Someone in the production office did a little research and discovered there was a troupe of 'little people' in Russia, working in a circus. That idea and research had taken a couple of days to produce a result, yet the ex-Line Producer had taken six months to come up with nothing...!

We discovered there were about thirty of them spread throughout Russia, and of course, upon hearing the word 'Russia', Paul looked at me and said, 'Lidia, that's your job.'

I connected with my production friends at Three T who said they knew how to find some of the group, so with that, I flew to Moscow. There were thirty-two of them, spread across the country, with one even living in Vladivostok – which is about as far south in Russia as you can get, and over 5,000 miles from Moscow.

We managed to gather them all in the capital to meet and interview (none of them spoke English), though they arrived with a sort of manager in tow, who spoke good English, particularly where money was concerned. He stated, 'I represent them all' as he puffed out his chest in a display of chauvinistic manliness.

'Every one of them? Even the one from Vladivostok?' I asked mischievously.

'Yes. I will fly with them to London. They will require $500 a day each, and I take 10% of that,' he announced in a well-rehearsed speech.

'Hmmm. Where did you get $500 from?' I asked.

'Oh, I spoke to your producer,' he said.

He had actually spoken with the producer Paul had been brought in to replace by Warner Bros., though she was still seemingly around serving out her notice period and being rather unhelpful.

'You do know she has no authority to make a deal with you,' I replied. 'I do not know what sort of deals you are used to getting for your clients, but $500? No...'

Whether he chose to ignore what I had just said, or whether it was the second part of his rehearsed speech I am not sure, but he continued dictating his terms:

'They will require bottled Evian water every day, fresh fruit every morning, three meals a day...'

'Look,' I interrupted. 'Meals are no problem, fruit I can get, I can even look into Evian water, but *you* are not coming to London and dictating financial terms like this.'

'Then you don't have your little people,' he grinned.

I said, 'Fine,' and ended the meeting.

I spoke to Inna, one of the little people whom I had grown friendly with throughout all this and asked her (in Russian) if he was really their agent.

'Sometimes he comes with some work and projects for us, sometimes he doesn't, but no, it is not like he is saying,' she explained.

I asked if she would do me a huge favour and speak to her colleagues, explain there was a minimum of six months' work in London, on very favourable terms, but *without* their self-appointed agent in tow. I knew if that chap came over, he would have been a total pain and extremely militant in his demands. Though, ironically, he was not so much concerned about his clients as his own pocket.

Inna came back saying they were actually incredibly happy, as this agent was taking a lot of money from them all the time, leaving them with very little of their true earnings.

Paul was in Chicago on a recce when I called him and was not at all happy when he heard about his predecessor interfering in negotiations – to the point she had actually sent an email, confirming the fees.

'What deal can you do?'

'Is it ok if I offered $250 per working day, accommodation, per diem and of course meals?' I asked. 'And as a consolation prize for the agent, can we offer him a couple of days in London, and then get rid of him?'

In the end, thirty-one of the lovely people came over – the guy from Vladivostok didn't want to, but then again, he seemed to pick and choose what projects he did with the others.

As the troupe spoke only a smattering of English between them, I thought it would be best to have a translator assigned exclusively to them in order that they would understand everything the director asked or suggested.

It just so happened Paul and I were having lunch at the Pinewood restaurant that day and one of the regular waitresses who served us, Releeka, had an Eastern European accent, so I asked whereabouts she came from.

'Russia,' she replied.

'We're looking for a translator and need someone on the set,' Paul smiled, 'and I think we might have just found her.'

Releeka was a very bright girl and spoke perfect English. She agreed to move into the hotel with our little people and be on call throughout the shoot. From waitressing on tables, she suddenly found herself working on a huge Hollywood movie with a hotel and a decent salary.

I checked out a couple of places that could accommodate all thirty-one, and near my home in West Drayton there was a little privately owned hotel which was extremely cute and had sixteen rooms – perfect for us, as they were all sharing. I had a chat with the manager and explained it would be a six-month block booking for his whole building by Warner Bros. – his eyes lit up

'Name it!' he said.

We agreed a price, but I added that I needed him to make some modifications, such as lowering rails in wardrobes, putting stools in the bathrooms, and in the kitchen area I asked if he would modify it so that our guests could reach the worktops to make snacks and drinks.

'No problem,' he affirmed.

Our little people had moved in before October 31st and no one had thought to tell them about Halloween; being a largely American tradition, the date meant nothing to them. But one night after filming, they became very distressed when they saw lots of people wearing masks and creepy costumes walking around outside the hotel.

The next day, Vince got to hear about it and declared they should all be moved to the Hilton in Park Lane, London. A glorious hotel, but not such a glorious idea as being a good hour by car (or coach) from Pinewood and very expensive, it wasn't very practical. But it made us more mindful about ensuring our visitors didn't get spooked again.

We hired a minibus for their weekends off and sent the troupe on outings, plus they took the local buses into Uxbridge on their days off. On workdays, they ate royally on set and took photographs to send home – it was all a wonderful, fun, adventure for them and they were really joyous to be around.

Ahead of flying over, Warner Bros. thought it would be hugely beneficial for some of the troupe to learn English, so we set up two schools – one in Minsk, and the other in Moscow. I chose the six most fluent English speaking to take part in the press junket all across the USA, ending up in LA for the premiere.

It was a really enjoyable experience for me, though Paul had headaches along the way as Vince Vaughn was very much calling the shots (as co-producer and star) and could be quite difficult. The director was lovely but was not a strong person, which led to issues, particularly when Paul was concerned that Vaughn could not be heard in some scenes when he watched the rushes back.

'I guess it'll be ok when we loop in post…' Paul suggested.

David Dobkin looked Paul squarely in the face, 'Vince will not do dubbing – he goes off script. He will not dub.'

Paul seemed quite deflated, as he always wanted to deliver the best possible film he could, though it seemed in this case he was being thwarted by its own star.

The usual question came in from Warner Bros. Namely: 'How can we reduce the budget?'

Paul had already sent a few emails saying he felt they were shooting far too much material, and that's when Joel Silver joined the project as another producer (to help reduce costs). Paul suggested to him that, as the script was quite episodic, a few scenes could easily be dropped without impacting the rest of the film.

'No, Vince Vaughn wants to shoot it as it is,' was the response that came back.

There was so much material that there was actually more footage left out of the film than there was in it. In fact, in order to hit the studio's self-imposed deadline of finishing in the UK before Christmas 2006, seven units were shooting simultaneously. Paul kept telling me that never before, not even on the biggest and most complicated action films, had he seen so many cameras and so much material coming into the editing rooms, but David Dobkin was emphatic the UK shoot, totally as scripted, needed to be completed in its entirety as they were scheduled to fly across the Atlantic in order to 'catch the snow in Chicago' immediately after the holidays.

Just ahead of the film's release, in November 2007, Queen Elizabeth visited Pinewood Studios to inaugurate the new entrance to the facility, subsequently dubbed the QE2 Gate. At a little reception afterwards, Her Majesty was introduced to senior management from the studio, and Paul was asked to join the line-up as one of the longest serving residents (he had been there 60 years from starting in the accounts department as a boy). Upon being introduced as one of the producers of *Fred Claus*, Her Majesty asked Paul if it was true that the fire on the 007 stage necessitated a move to Cardington. Paul, being somewhat taken aback by the monarch's knowledge, was further impressed when the Queen began to talk about the airships she had visited there in her youth.

The film was released a few weeks later, in time for Christmas, but fared poorly with critics and audiences alike, failing to make its $100m budget back.

I am afraid that was it for Paul. It had been an unhappy experience and one he did not want to repeat. He stated he had had enough and would never make another Hollywood studio movie.

***

There were a few scripts that Paul championed, plus books he had read and sought finance for as a consultant post-*Fred Claus*, though, of course, without studio backing, you are continually financing all your own running costs and it becomes incredibly expensive. Yes, there were one or two projects that got close, but ultimately never quite made it over the line.

In 2010, after three years of developing and seeking backing, Paul decided that he really wanted to pack it all in. My career had become so interlinked with his that there really was no question of me working with anyone else, so we both announced our retirement – once and for all.

CHAPTER 18

Paul

As I mentioned earlier, I first met Paul Hitchcock during Barbra Streisand's recce in Prague in 1982, when Warner Bros. were involved in the picture, and his claims of declaring his love to me on a napkin at dinner seemed quite ludicrous. I do believe that there is such a thing as love at first sight, as clichéd as it may sound, but I never expected to see Paul again in any event.

Crossing paths with different 'foreigner producers' was part of my job; when they arrived in Prague to explore production opportunities, we would work together quite closely for a week or two and strike up friendships. That is how I got to know Peter Lamont, for example, who became such a good friend and help when I needed to get Frank work in England.

But visiting filmmakers were rarely around long enough for any serious relationships to develop; in fact, many said, 'we nearly have all the money, and we'll be back soon' but never in fact returned. Then there were others who did have finance locked in but did not return either – perhaps because they had found alternative locations nearer to home, or perhaps because it was not what the director had envisioned.

It struck me that a lot of American and British producers did not seem terribly comfortable in Czechoslovakia, as aside from (feared and mysterious) communist rule, there was a shortage of top hotels or decent food, and it's fair to say a lot of the locals wore drab-looking grey or brown clothes and were pretty miserable. To be honest, it wasn't a terribly appealing place in which to spend months away from home!

The latter was certainly the case with director Richard Donner and his movie *Ladyhawke*.

In 1983 Paul returned to Prague – I had learned better English by then too! – and having experienced the city before, he struck me as being pretty serious about filming; but although Paul knew my country, it was a new experience for Dick Donner – and one he was seemingly not keen to prolong. You see, Dick had a specific image in his mind for his movie of an imposing hilltop castle – and one thing Czechoslovakia isn't short of is castles! We travelled wide and far, visiting many, including some in Moravia over in the east of the country, where we found one which Dick declared 'perfect'. We went inside to explore further and I do not know if he spoke to someone or saw mention of something, but Dick came over to me and asked, bluntly: 'Lidia, this castle was recently used in a film with Klaus Kinski wasn't it?'

I admitted that it had been, though I was not sure why it might be an issue. Dick said, 'I am not using it then.' He was adamant that he would not re-use someone else's set, regardless of the fact the castle had been standing for hundreds of years and been seen by hundreds of thousands of people.

Dick's character was very 'Los Angeles' in that he was gregarious, larger than life, full of energy and enjoyed the very finest of everything. I had already got the distinct impression that he did not care much for the hotels, the restaurants, the food, nor the scarcity of everyday items, which all conspired to constrain him. Prague was the polar opposite of everything he was used to in LA. The castle visit seemed to be the excuse he was looking for and he immediately announced he was going to take one of the unit cars to Vienna, which was about two and a half hours drive. He literally got in and instructed the driver to 'go' and did not even return to his hotel to pack.

'I'll see you back in London,' were his parting words to Paul, who stood looking crestfallen and confused, having sold Dick on the benefits of shooting in Czechoslovakia. Paul took the very public rejection very personally; despite his outward appearance of being a tough movie producer, Paul was a sensitive soul who valued friendships highly and he honestly thought he and Dick – up until that point at any rate – were set to work together again (after *Superman*), and in Prague.

I had greatly enjoyed our couple of weeks working together, and after we packed everything up, Paul suggested that ahead of him leaving the next morning, I might go to the hotel to join him for breakfast, by way of a 'thank you'. I had loved being in his company over the previous weeks and found him to be a charming gentleman who loved to tell stories about movies and film stars. He was also incredibly interesting, knowledgeable, and well-read. Yet as outgoing as he was, I could not help but notice a sadness in his eyes.

I accepted his breakfast invitation and duly arrived around 8am, but could not see any of them in the restaurant, and after a little while I asked reception if Paul had checked out early, worried I had mixed up the time.

'No, he's still here in the hotel,' came the answer.

I asked if they would phone Paul's room, but there wasn't a reply.

'I'll go up and knock on his door,' I told the receptionist. 'Because he's going to miss his plane if he doesn't leave soon.'

I went upstairs, wondering to myself what had happened because he did seem upset when Dick Donner departed so suddenly, and rattled on Paul's door several times to no avail. I pressed down on the handle and noticed it was unlocked, so I pushed the door open and called inside – but there was no response.

I ventured into the semi-darkened room and could see he was in bed.

'Paul!' I exclaimed in a panicked tone, as I pulled the curtains open, 'you have a plane to catch! You shouldn't still be in here.' I thought he had overslept, but he lifted his head slightly from the pillow, sighed and dropped it down again. I couldn't understand what had happened to turn the fun, energetic and bubbly man I had known a couple of days before into the man who now looked as though he'd had the stuffing knocked out of him.

'I can help you to pack. Your car will be here soon,' I suggested, trying to provoke some sense of urgency, but he just lay there, staring at the wall.

I could see he was still breathing at least, and still conscious, but he seemed totally emotionless and disinterested in anything I said. After my pointless efforts to stir him verbally, I asked if I could use his bathroom. He grunted a sort of 'yeah'.

Moments later, I returned and slipped into the bed beside him.

I had started to develop feelings for Paul, and seeing him in that depressed and emotionless state really brought them to the fore – I was genuinely concerned he might be having some sort of breakdown and, realising it might possibly be the last time I ever saw him, I felt I needed to be close to him, to hold him and to comfort him.

Our closeness led us to make the most wonderful love, and the Paul I had known and began to fall for was suddenly back. But there was no time for romance! I told him he must quickly pack his things as he had a plane to catch. I honestly thought that was 'goodbye' as he certainly would not be returning with *Ladyhawke*. In the event, Dick Donner settled on shooting in Italy.

***

Shortly afterwards Paul called up and invited me to visit him in Austria, but I said it was simply not possible for me to travel to a Western country. He did not really understand, and he seemed taken aback when I spelled out how we were effectively imprisoned 'behind barbed wire' in Czechoslovakia and how tightly our movements were limited by the communist regime. Only then did he begin to appreciate just how repressed and controlled we were.

A few phone conversations ensued, and he kindly sent Martin some vinyl albums that had just been released in the UK. That aside, I honestly consigned our romance to being one of those wonderful things that, well, was a one-off.

Three or four months later, Paul called again to say he was about to start work on a Warner Bros. movie in Austria and, realising it was close to Czechoslovakia and possibly easier for me to travel there, asked if I would be able to meet him. I explained that visiting Austria or Italy, for a communist citizen, would encounter a barrage of questions from the authorities. However, I suggested that we could meet in Bratislava – now the capital city of Slovakia – which was less than an hour from Vienna, and up until 1993 was part of Czechoslovakia. It was quite a long train journey, several hours from Prague, but perfectly doable and more importantly, it would be a trip that would not cause any awkward questions from my superiors.

Paul was elated, and we agreed our rendezvous, though I laughed when he said he had to be sure to buy a case of Czech beer.

'But you don't drink beer,' I exclaimed when we met up and saw Paul loading it into his car.

'No, but Clint Eastwood does, and he said, "When you go to meet your Czech lady, would you bring me some back?".'

We met a few times during 1984 whilst Paul was shooting, including on a trip he made to Prague under the pretext of doing a recce for another possible movie. It was always difficult saying goodbye each time as we never knew if it might be the last.

Paul told me all about his life and how, in 1952, after his National Service, he had returned to his job in the accounts department at Pinewood Studios where he was soon promoted to the budgeting division, learning about film costings and scheduling. He was in a 9-5, fairly safe job for the parent company of the studio, The Rank Organisation, but Paul was ambitious and wanted to progress his career so in the early 1960s he saw his chance to branch out as a freelancer: earning more money – which his wife Beryl liked – though it meant him being away from home for long spells on location and attending industry functions – which Beryl didn't like.

He never bullshitted me. In fact, he said, 'Although my marriage is not good, I will never leave Beryl.'

I admired his honesty.

Though the more we chatted the more I realised he always spoke about his marriage in the past tense: it seemed clear they had grown apart long before Paul met me. Having been in an unhappy marriage myself, and one we kept the façade of purely for our son's sake, I knew all too well how Paul was feeling and despite being surrounded by production colleagues, just how lonely he seemed.

I was not looking for anything long-term, nor would I have asked anything more of Paul than the fun time we had together; I was divorced, single and had a clear conscience.

In 1985, Paul had filming assignments in far-flung parts of the world and I was beginning to prepare my escape. In prioritising my and Martin's future life, I deliberately cooled communication with Paul, as it was the safest thing for all.

Once we had settled in London, I did phone Paul, just to let him know we were safe, but never saw him until 1990 at Pinewood. I know he felt hurt and confused as to why I had broken off contact and had to wait several years to find out why – hence him being so surprised to see me in his office that day at Pinewood when I popped over from the Weintraub library.

We rekindled our friendship, and that is when Paul confided that he had, several years earlier, left his wife Beryl after falling in love. He set up an apartment with his new lady in central London, but Beryl had turned up one day in a terrible state and, using their children as pawns (they had a son and a daughter), threatened that Paul would never see them again, unless he returned home. She even threatened to kill herself and said it would 'leave the children without a mother' and it would all be Paul's fault.

The guilt and anguish were unbearable for Paul. He ended his relationship, sold his flat (at a significant loss) and moved back to be with Beryl. All in the name of the children.

For her part, Beryl promised to take more interest in his work – that lasted for six months. She hated the film business, hated socialising and although she enjoyed the financial rewards it brought, she told Paul she never wanted anyone from his work to visit their house.

In 1989, Paul was making a film with his favourite director, Clint Eastwood, entitled *White Hunter, Black Heart* and part of the shoot took place at Pinewood Studios. After lunching with Clint a few times in the studio restaurant, and him being constantly badgered by people wanting to say hello, the star asked Paul if there was somewhere else they could have lunch in future. Paul suggested his local pub in Stoke Poges, where he introduced Clint to a 'ploughman's lunch'. During one of their many conversations at the pub, Clint asked Paul just how local to his house they were – Paul said, 'You see that roof across the car park – that's my house.'

'Is your wife in?' Clint asked.

Paul hesitated. 'Probably, yes.'

'I would like to meet her. Why don't you call her and invite her to join us?'

Paul said she would probably be busy, but Clint was insistent and so he made a call asking if Beryl would like to join him and Clint Eastwood. She snapped, 'No, I'm doing the laundry today.'

When I started working for Paul, we shared occasional lunches, dinners and outings and developed an extraordinarily strong friendship. It was no secret around the studio that Paul was in an unhappy marriage but as I have already said, from the outset with me, he was very up front, honest, and said that he would never leave his wife.

Although we stayed together whilst on location, to preserve decorum and propriety I always booked two rooms in hotels – usually adjoining, mind you – and ensured that from the time of leaving each morning until returning in the evening that everything was kept very businesslike and professional between us. I certainly did not want to embarrass Paul in any way nor compromise his authority on the production. I felt we were so discreet and careful that no one knew about us.

During the period when I was working for Stanley Kubrick, the director came over to my desk one Friday and asked, 'You are still seeing Paul Hitchcock, aren't you?'

I was quite mortified, until finally coughing, 'Well, yes, sort of.'

'Would you deliver this letter to him?' Stanley asked, nonplussed.

As I was with Stanley Monday through Saturday, I realised my only opportunity would be on a Sunday, so I called Paul to ask if I could drop it by his house.

'You must come to tea with us,' Paul kindly suggested.

It was a lovely sunny day, and after Beryl came to serve us, she stood up, saying she was busy. Paul asked that she stay to chat with me, but she curtly declined. Just before she moved away from the table, Beryl hesitated, turned around and looked me squarely in the eye.

'Would you like to see the garden?' she asked me.

Being polite, I readily agreed and genuinely marvelled at Beryl's green fingers and her huge, colourful display of flowers.

'You know there are rumours at Pinewood about you and Paul having an affair,' she said, quite casually and almost dismissive in tone. I was gobsmacked and dumbstruck, but in the few seconds that followed – whilst I was frantically struggling for something to say – Beryl actually replied for me, albeit extremely coldly:

'I do not think so! He is 60 years old and men at 60 do not have sex!' she laughed.

That one sentence confirmed to me just what sort of woman she was and what sort of marriage Paul had with her.

I returned to the table, feeling extremely uncomfortable and – if honest – quite angry at what I'd just heard. I left the letter for Paul and made my excuses to leave, all the way home thinking about how Paul had brushed off how his marriage was not a happy one, and just how much of an understatement it had been. The humiliation he must have felt in trying not to give Beryl any cause to disrupt her home life by insisting our relationship could never go beyond what it was, gave me a deeper appreciation for Paul. I had no wish to be a marriage wrecker – but then again, there was no marriage to wreck.

Paul did tell me that he didn't sleep in the same bedroom as his wife, and I knew he was telling me the truth.

***

He was always very conscientious, and quite often when I was assisting him at the office he would be on the phone to Los Angeles or picking up faxes into the early evening; even sometimes up until even 8pm or 9pm. I was waiting to leave of course, as was his right-hand man, Steve Harding, but we did not feel able to until our 'boss' said he'd finished for the day. It became more and more noticeable that Paul was finding extra things to do in the office, even after we had crossed all the T's and dotted all the I's twice over, and he used any little excuse to stay back.

He used to repeat a phrase the actor Peter Finch had once said to him: 'A happy man is someone who looks forward to going to work but also looks forward to going home at the end of the day.'

It was then I twigged – he was delaying going home. He did not want to go home. His children were by then grown up and had left, and his life with Beryl had become miserable. But he said he would never leave her again. Whilst she may have had her suspicions about me, it was her that Paul returned to every night.

You can imagine his surprise one evening in 2009 when she told Paul that there would be a letter coming the next morning from her solicitor.

'Solicitor?' Paul asked. 'What sort of letter?'

'You will see,' she replied.

The next day, the postman delivered a divorce petition. Paul couldn't quite believe that, despite being so unhappy, he had stayed with Beryl because it was what she said she wanted and now… now… it suited her to end things in a cold, impersonal way. He called his best friend, Ted, and asked if they could meet, but Ted admitted he could not as he had appointments all day.

'Ted. PLEASE. Meet me,' Paul pleaded.

Needless to say, Ted dropped everything and Paul showed him the letter.

'You are living a nightmare. You are not happy; she is obviously not happy. Don't fight it,' Ted reasoned.

Paul agreed, and within a year, the decree absolute was granted.

Meanwhile, Paul asked if I would help him search for an apartment and gave me the specifics of what he was looking for. I duly contacted all the local agents in the Pinewood area (where Paul had lived for years) and drew up a shortlist, but Paul – obviously realising he needed a clean break – said no, he wanted me to search further afield and away from where he might bump into his ex-wife.

'Nothing in this area. Maybe Ascot, Windsor or Sunningdale,' he suggested.

Again, I drew up a shortlist, and there was one in Ascot that ticked all the boxes. I went to see what was a lovely apartment block in huge private grounds with every mod con. Paul came over to view it and loved it, and aside from a few cosmetic things he wanted to change, he declared it ideal.

A deal was made and Paul arranged to move in. I will forever remember him pulling up in his car outside the front of his new home, after I'd collected the keys, and emerging with just a suitcase. I looked around, expecting a van to be following, but no, that was it – he had arrived with what he could fit in the back seat of his Bentley. (Much like I had arrived in London for the first time).

'I just wanted to get out. I have been treated worse than a dog,' he said tearfully. Beryl had turned everyone against him, to the point his daughter did not speak to him for six long years, his grandchildren ostracised him, and though his son maintained contact, it was all very difficult and fraught.

He never had any personal effects – no bedding, towels, pots, pans or cutlery.

'She can have everything,' he told me.

We started making a shopping list and off I went…

Although I was living in my own home, I realised that Paul could not survive living on his own – it was not that he could not shop or cook (though then again, at least Beryl did that much), it was more that Paul had such a sociable personality that he needed company. He needed people around, so I started visiting once or twice a week, which became three or four times a week… to the point when I moved in. That was in 2011.

On Valentine's Day that year Paul proposed to me, but cautioned that – although he did not care what Beryl or his family thought – he wanted to leave it a year, as he did not want it to appear as if we were marrying on the rebound. He was thinking more about me than himself.

I was so happy, and of course, I said a long engagement was not an issue!

In 2012, we held our marriage ceremony in Portugal, which we preceded with a civil marriage in Windsor – in the very same room where King Charles married Queen Camilla seven years earlier. The 'wedding party' in Portugal was so beautiful and full of joy, with seventy-five guests in an elegant garden setting; it was both our second marriages, so neither of us wanted anything too flashy or gauche!

Having gone from being a production assistant on *Yentl* in Prague during his first recce, to becoming Paul's assistant in London and then on to becoming Mrs Hitchcock… it was my happiest of Hollywood endings.

***

Paul and I were the best of friends who chatted about everything and anything, and one day I asked him, 'What do you think went wrong in your first marriage?'

He looked at me and said quite sadly, 'Honestly?... I do not think I really ever loved Beryl, though I did respect her as the mother of our children.'

We never spoke about her again.

CHAPTER 19

It's A Wrap!

Paul and I were amazingly comfortable together. We talked all the time about everything and anything and laughed so much. There was never a dull moment. I learned so much from him about the finer things in life, including appreciating gourmet food, fine wine and five-star hotels such as the Gritti Palace in Venice, Le Negresco in Nice and Hotel Du Lac in Zurich. I flew first class and in private jets, which was all quite alien to me, being from a very modest background in Prague. Though that is not to say Paul wasn't just as happy sitting with his feet up in front of the TV at home with a sandwich, because he was.

Paul was so modest and so thoughtful because if we were in a fancy restaurant and I looked unsure about anything on the menu, I could quietly ask 'what's this' and Paul would explain gently and without causing me any embarrassment. To be honest, it was not just fancy food, but things like fish – back home we would have carp or trout, whereas now I was being offered all sorts from Dover sole to John Dory, red snapper, and bluefin tuna. Paul always encouraged me to ask if I was unsure, as he loved introducing people to new dishes and was regarded as such a culinary expert that Clint Eastwood dubbed him European eating champion! That was certainly true when it came to Italian food.

The only time I ever felt intimidated was when we were in LA once and Paul booked a birthday dinner for me at L'Orangerie, which specialised in French haute cuisine – although it later closed in 2006 (and was sold to Nobu). For almost 30 years, it was one of *the* places to eat in California. Upon entering the huge ornate conservatory-type room, resplendent with painted murals, palm trees and gold leaf adornments, and even though I had my absolute best dress on, I felt completely underdressed. The clientele was probably the richest in LA, with jewellery that you usually only ever see on the Oscars red carpet, just to have dinner. I felt conscious that I did not belong there, and I cannot recall anything about the meal, just that I was glad to get out of there. It certainly kept me grounded, and Paul often chuckled about it.

***

In his final years, my darling Paul suffered two strokes; the second of which in 2019 was described as being 'serious' and resulted in him losing vision in one eye.

Despite the very best surgeon and consultant's help, Paul was told, unfortunately, he would never regain vision in the eye and he took it in his usual so brave and stoic manner; despite knowing he wouldn't be able to drive again or enjoy the movies or football matches he so loved visiting ever the same again.

Over time, as elements of his independence were slowly eroded, his disability began noticeably affecting him both physically and mentally. One day, I could see he was worried about something, and he asked me, 'Lidia, what will happen if we cannot have sex anymore?'

'Paul! If our love is based only on sex, then that is dreadful,' I replied.

He smiled and squeezed my hand.

Having celebrated his 91st birthday, and despite the aches and pains of advancing years, Paul and I still enjoyed an incredibly happy and full life together. Tragically, that all changed suddenly in the spring of 2023 when he fell over in the garden and needed surgery to repair and pin his hip. He died three days after the operation – the trauma was too much for his body.

Things have never been the same for me since, and never will be again.

In 2024, the management at Pinewood Studios kindly suggested they would like to arrange a memorial and tree planting for Paul in the gardens, overlooking his longtime office in the Warner Bros. bungalow.

It was an emotional day with many friends and colleagues joining me to pay tribute, share some stories and raise a glass. It was a wonderful day full of laughter and love. I often visit the tree, smile, and think of our times together and of how lucky I have been.

Although I consider myself to be British through and through, I still visit Prague and marvel at the freedoms young people there have and indeed take for granted. They are so lucky. I am so lucky. Of course, I will always be emotionally attached to the Czech Republic, but my life will forever be in the UK where my son and grandchildren live… and where my life with Paul was.

It has been one hell of a journey – some say it reads like a Hollywood script. I wonder who might play me in the film?!

FILMOGRAPHY

1976 – 1985 Production Manager/Production Assistant Barrandov Film Studios, Prague, on scores of Czech and Russian films.

From 1982 assigned to international co-productions including *Yentl*, and international directors and film technicians on recces such as to production designer Peter Lamont on *Octopussy* (1983).

1986-1990 Various (non-film) roles in and around London including working for BBC World Service.

1990 – 1991 Secretary at Weintraub Film Library, Pinewood Studios.

1991 Engaged by Warner Bros. for an unmade Jiří Menzel project and then assigned to various projects in development including *The Aryan Papers* (unmade, Stanley Kubrick).

1991 onwards Executive Assistant to the Producer/Production Manager/Unit Manager:
The Life and Extraordinary Adventures of Private Ivan Chonkin (1994)
Terminal Velocity (1994)
First Knight (1995)
Mission: Impossible (1996)
The Saint (1997)
The Man In The Iron Mask (1998)
Vertical Limit (2000)
M:i2 (2000)

Cast Away (2000)
Vertical Limit (2000) [reshoot]

Providing product placement on films, including:
Ronin (1998)
M:i2 (2000)
Bridget Jones' Diary (2001)
Lara Croft: Tomb Raider (2001)
And Now Ladies And Gentlemen (2002)
Die Another Day (2002)
Lara Croft: The Cradle of Life [Tomb Raider 2] (2003)
Phantom of the Opera (2004)
Layer Cake (2004)
Wimbledon (2004)
Alfie (2004)
Batman Begins (2005)
Casino Royale (2006)
Mission: Impossible 3 (2006)

2007 *Fred Claus* (Executive Assistant to the Producer, Warner Bros.)

2008 – 2009 Freelance work on various productions in development.

ACKNOWLEDGEMENTS

I wanted to write this memoir for some time, but instead I encouraged my late husband to write a book with stories from behind the scenes. As a matter of fact, I wrote a script about my escape in 1986, but that was a complete fabrication except the part of the escape. My then partner wanted it to be scandalous story and I did not agree, so it is gathering dust in the loft.

I said to myself, if I ever write this memoir, it has to be truth, nothing but the truth and here we are now with this true version of my life so far.

I want to give huge thanks to:

My late husband, Paul, who made the second half of my life so rewarding, filled it full of fun and love – I owe him so very much, and dedicate this book to him.

My son Martin, whose youthful bravery allowed us to live the most wonderful lives.

Gareth Owen, for his belief that my story was one worth telling, and for helping me craft it into this book.

My wonderful publisher, for their immediate and wonderful enthusiasm, and for wanting to join me on the exciting journey into print.

My editor, James Shaw.

Robin Harbour, for casting his good eye over the manuscript, and Damian Fox for his keen eye too.

And finally, a thanks to the friends, colleagues, crews and stars who have been a part of my life – and particularly Barbra Streisand for opening my eyes.

www.ingramcontent.com/pod-product-compliance
Lightning Source LLC
LaVergne TN
LVHW041616070426
835507LV00008B/270